ultimate

weird but true

2

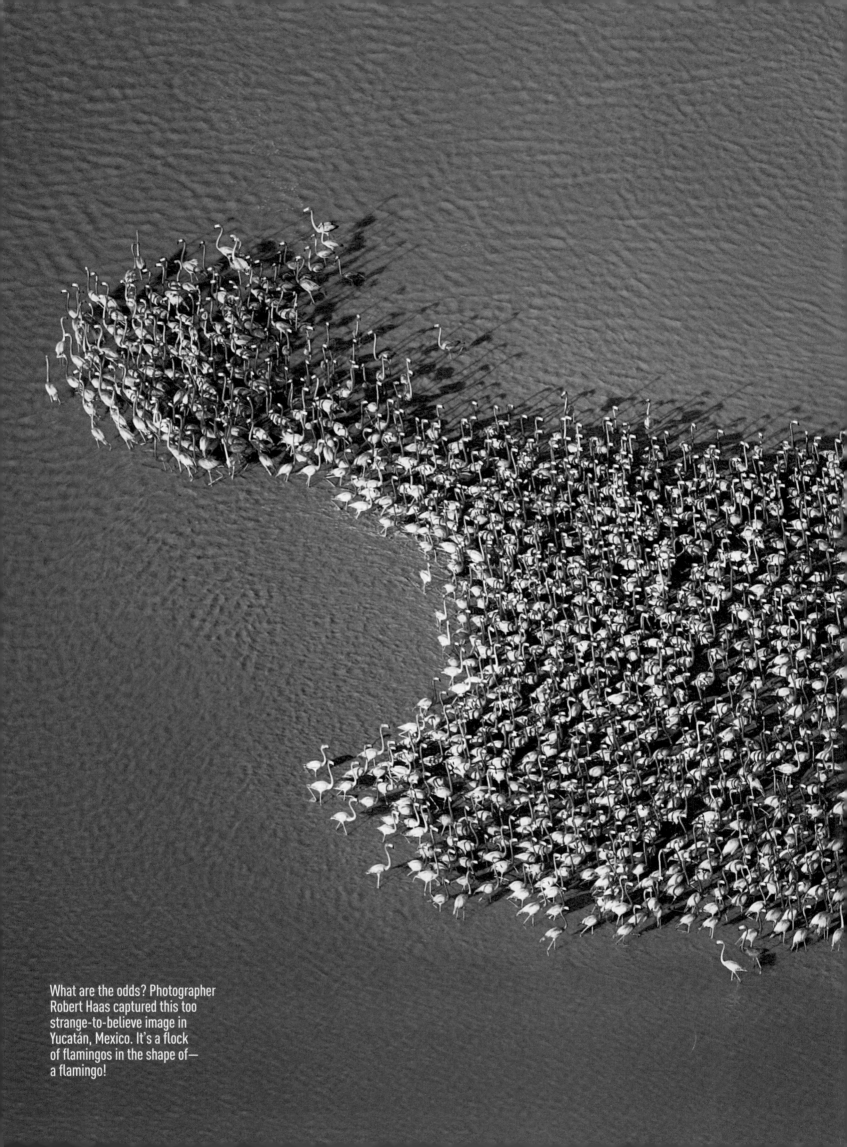

What are the odds? Photographer Robert Haas captured this too strange-to-believe image in Yucatán, Mexico. It's a flock of flamingos in the shape of— a flamingo!

ultimate

weird but true

2

NATIONAL GEOGRAPHIC SOCIETY

WASHINGTON, D.C.

contents

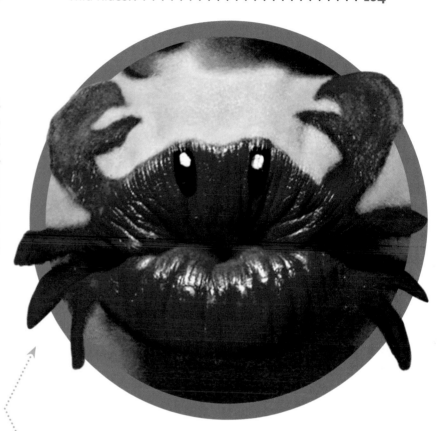

Norman's Facebook page has over **7,000** likes.

Norman the scooter-riding dog also has a YouTube channel. Check out more awesome animals on page 8.

eXTREME WEiRDNESS

Cow Jumper >>>

NAME: Luna

SPECIAL TALENT:
Luna "**moo-ves**" more like a horse than a cow. With her owner riding on her back, this well-balanced bovine can **leap** over **logs** and hoof it over hurdles.

FUN FACT:
Luna also responds to the **commands** "Go," "Stand," and "Gallop."

They've Got TaLENT

Scooter Dog!

NAME: Norman

SPECIAL TALENT: Norman has been **riding** his family's scooter since he was a puppy. He also likes to skateboard and ride a bike around his neighborhood.

FUN FACT: Norman is a breed of French **herding dog** called a **briard.**

NAMES: Alia, Nastia, and Kelia

SPECIAL TALENT:
This clever **trio** blows **giant bubbles** underwater—all at the **same time!**

FUN FACT:
These belugas can also **catch balls** in their mouths and jump through **hoops.**

Bubble-Blowing Whales

NAME: Marsha

SPECIAL TALENT:
Marsha **paints** colorful pictures with her nose and her pointy **upper lip.**

FUN FACT:
Marsha's **masterpieces** have been featured in an **art show** and are also sold in the gift shop of the zoo where she lives.

Surfing Goat

Rhino Artist

NAME: Pismo

SPECIAL TALENT:
This California **kid** rides **the waves** alongside his human friends.

FUN FACT:
Pismo and his mother, Goatee, even have their own **Facebook page!**

NAME: Mog

SPECIAL TALENT:
Water doesn't phase this **fearless** feline. Mog makes a **splash** swimming laps for 15 minutes every week.

FUN FACT:
Mog was completely **paralyzed** after being **hit by a car,** but **swimming** has made him strong enough to walk again.

Swimming Cat

NAME: Nung Ning

SPECIAL TALENT: This **pachyderm** plays **basketball** by standing on her hind legs and using her trunk to **"shoot" hoops.**

FUN FACT: Elephants at a rescue center for the animals in Thailand, where Nung Ning lives, also **dance** for visitors.

Elephant Hoops

LEAP
OF
FAiTH

HIS HELMET HAD BUILT-IN EARPHONES AND A MICROPHONE, SO HE COULD COMMUNICATE WITH PEOPLE ON THE GROUND.

WITHOUT THIS SPECIAL PRESSURIZED SUIT, BAUMGARTNER'S BODY FLUIDS WOULD BEGIN TO BOIL ABOVE 61,000 FEET (18,593 m).

FastFACTS

JUMPER'S NAME: Felix Baumgartner

RECORD-SETTING JUMP: 127,852 feet (38,969 m)

WHERE: From the stratosphere to Earth

SPEED: 843.6 mph (1357.6 km/h)—faster than a passenger jet

GOING UP: A giant helium balloon carried Baumgartner to his jumping-off point.

THE SUIT WAS MODELED AFTER THOSE WORN BY PILOTS OF HIGH-ALTITUDE SPY PLANES.

THE STRATOSPHERE IS THE LAYER OF THE ATMOSPHERE BETWEEN SIX AND THIRTY MILES (9.7 AND 38.2 km) ABOVE THE EARTH.

3, 2, 1 JUMP!

How long does it take to fall 24 miles (39 km)? For "Fearless Felix," the entire descent took only nine minutes. He went supersonic—dropping at 843.6 miles an hour (1357.6 km/h)—and became the first person to break the sound barrier in a free fall! Baumgartner's parachute opened as planned about a mile and a half (2.4 km) above the ground, and he landed safely in a desert in New Mexico, U.S.A.

This man broke the speed of sound in a free fall from 24 MILES (39 km) above Earth!

BiG BiTES

SUPER FRIED RICE

WHAT IT IS: A heaping helping of fried rice prepared by 30 chefs at a food fair in Thailand

WEIGHS IN AT: Over 1,500 pounds (680 kg)

FOOD FOR THOUGHT: This staggering stir-fry could fill 1,400 take-out boxes.

GIANT OMELETTE

WHAT IT IS: An "eggs-treme" truffle omelette made for a mushroom festival in Croatia

WEIGHS IN AT: 243 pounds (110 kg)

FOOD FOR THOUGHT: It would take a chicken almost eight years to lay the more than 2,000 eggs needed to make this omelette.

COLOSSAL CAKE

WHAT IT IS: A four-layer, five-story-tall wedding cake created for a trade show in the Philippines

WEIGHS IN AT: 11,200 pounds (5,080 kg)

FOOD FOR THOUGHT:
This cake could be sliced into 18,000 servings!

MEGA BURGER

WHAT IT IS: A $400 burger made with 160 slices of cheese, 5 onions, 12 tomatoes, and 33 pickles!

WEIGHS IN AT: 123 pounds (56 kg)

FOOD FOR THOUGHT:
The burger is big enough to feed some 100 people!

Don't Try This AT HOME

DAVID **"THE BULLET" SMITH** HAS BEEN **SHOT OUT** OF **A CANNON** MORE THAN **5,000** TIMES, **AND HAS SOARED UP** TO **77 FEET** (23 m) IN THE **AIR.**

THIS MOSCOW STATE CIRCUS **STRONGMAN PULLED** A **DOUBLE-DECKER BUS** USING ONLY HIS **TEETH.**

WINGWALKERS PERFORM **FLIPS** ON **TOP** OF **AIRPLANES** WHILE **FLYING** UP TO **150** MILES (241 km/h) **AN HOUR!**

THIS MAN'S NECK IS SO **STRONG** HE CAN BALANCE A **363-POUND** (165-kg) **QUAD BIKE** ON HIS HEAD!

HOW **LOW** CAN SHE **GO?** THIS **AMAZING ROLLER SKATER GLIDES UNDER POLES** THAT ARE LESS THAN A FOOT (28 cm) **OFF THE GROUND.**

BULLS-EYE! THIS **SUPER-BENDY WOMAN** CAN **SHOOT A BOW** AND **ARROW** WITH HER **FEET**— WHILE DOING AN ELEVATED **HANDSTAND!**

Professional **surfer** GARRETT McNAMARA rode a monster wave* as TALL as a TEN-STORY BUILDING— setting a world record!

Some **monster waves** can travel **faster** than a **speeding car** and pack enough **power to tear a ship in half.**

ultimate secret revealed!

How does a wave become a monster? Also called rogue waves, these walls of water come out of stormy areas of the ocean and can tower more than 100 feet (30 m) tall. The supersize waves occur when several smaller waves join to form giants. The relatively large number of observations of rogue waves is a surprise for experts.

Monster waves have been known to swallow entire ships, so how did McNamara survive this wild ride? A friend towed him out to the wave on a Jet Ski, accelerating to the same speed as the wave before McNamara hopped on. Then the surfer hung on for the ride of his life!

9 Wacky FACTS

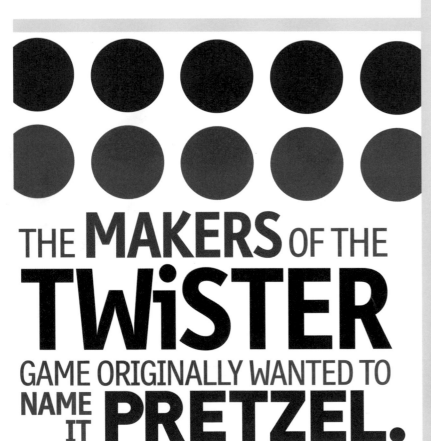

PLAY-DOH WAS **ORIGINALLY** USED TO **CLEAN WALLPAPER.**

THE **MAKERS** OF THE **TWISTER** GAME ORIGINALLY WANTED TO **NAME** IT **PRETZEL.**

YOU CAN **COMBINE** **SiX** LEGO **BRICKS** INTO **915,103,765** **DiFFERENT SHAPES.**

TOYS ARE **BANNED** IN **KiDS' MEALS** AT **FAST FOOD** RESTAURANTS IN **CHILE.**

ABOUT FUN

THE WORLD'S **LARGEST MONOPOLY** GAME BOARD IS **LARGER** THAN A **THREE-CAR** GARAGE.

ILLINOIS AVENUE

INDIANA AVENUE

BADMiNTON WAS ONCE CALLED BATTLEDORE.

NORWAY RECOGNIZES THE **ViDEO GAME "DANCE DANCE REVOLUTION"** AS AN OFFICIAL **SPORT.**

A CANADIAN MAN **BANGED** ON THE **DRUMS** FOR MORE THAN **26 HOURS** WHILE PLAYING THE VIDEO GAME "**ROCK BAND.**"

5,000-YEAR-OLD **DOLLS** WERE FOUND IN **EGYPTiAN GRAVES.**

ANIMAL MaSH-UPS!

PIZZLY BEAR

MASH-UP: Polar Bear + Grizzly Bear

BIZARRE BLEND: This bear has the lighter coloring of a polar bear with the face and humpback of a grizzly. A very rare occurrence in the wild, pizzlies typically are the result of the two species living together in captivity.

PIZZLY BEAR

POLAR BEAR + GRIZZLY BEAR

GEEP

MASH-UP: Goat + Sheep

BIZARRE BLEND: Her dad is a billy goat. Her mom is a ewe. The result? This geep's got a sheep's build with a goat's brown coat and long, agile legs.

GOAT + SHEEP = GEEP

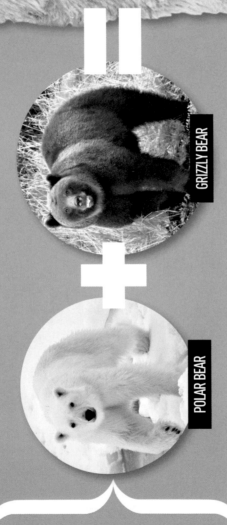

WHOLPIN

MASH-UP: False Killer Whale + Bottlenose Dolphin

BIZARRE BLEND: One of only a few known wholphins in the world, this mixed-up mammal's mom is a bottlenose dolphin and its dad is a false killer whale. Born in captivity, this wholphin weighs 600 pounds (272 kg) and measures nearly 10 feet (3 m) long—halfway between its petite mom and giant dad!

WHOLPIN

BOTTLENOSE DOLPHIN

FALSE KILLER WHALE

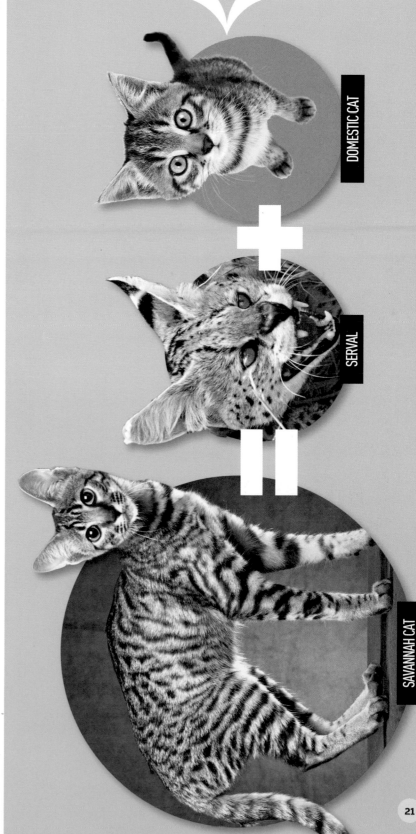

SAVANNAH CAT

MASH-UP: Domestic Cat + Serval (a type of wildcat)

BIZARRE BLEND: It can cost $20,000 to adopt one of these fancy felines, which can grow to more than twice the size of normal cats and can be trained to play fetch! These beauties are bred to be pets, but they are illegal in some places for fear that they could alter the ecosystem if they got loose in the wild.

DOMESTIC CAT

SERVAL

SAVANNAH CAT

Octopush

SPECIAL GEAR:
Snorkeling gear, small stick, and a puck

WHY IT'S WEIRD:
It's just like regular hockey, except that the game is played underwater at the bottom of a swimming pool!

World's STRANGEST Sports

Pogo-Sticking

SPECIAL GEAR:
Pogo stick with extra-bouncy springs

WHY IT'S WEIRD:
Jumpers bound up to 9.5 feet (2.9 m) in the air—high enough to pogo over a Porsche.

Bossaball

SPECIAL GEAR:
Trampoline, volleyball net, and ball

WHY IT'S WEIRD:
Volleyball meets soccer meets gymnastics in this high-flying game. Players leap and flip on a trampoline while hitting and kicking the ball over the net.

Extreme Urban Climbing

SPECIAL GEAR:
No fear

WHY IT'S WEIRD:
Thrill seekers clamber up the sides of **buildings**—some **70 stories high!**—without the help of climbing gear or a safety harness. They aren't just risking their lives—they're risking being **arrested.** The sport is **illegal** in many places.

SPECIAL GEAR:
A **fishing pole** and tons of **muscle**

WHY IT'S WEIRD:
It can take **30 minutes** and the strength of **two people** to reel in these **supersize** catfish, some weighing more than a grown man!

Monster Fishing

SPECIAL GEAR:
High-heeled shoes

WHY IT'S WEIRD:
Runners sprint—or **teeter**—to the finish line in a race to see who's **fastest,** and who has the best **balance.**

High-Heel Racing

Elephant Polo

SPECIAL GEAR:
Extra-long polo stick, ball, and an **elephant**

WHY IT'S WEIRD:
Most polo players ride horses up and down the field. But in this game, players ride **pachyderms** instead, using **superlong sticks** to strike the ball and score goals.

23

Some **people's** **SNORES** are **AS LOUD** as a **vacuum** cleaner!

24

The **loudest** snores can reach more than **100 DECiBELS.**

That's also **as loud as** the sound of highway traffic, a power mower, or **a tractor!**

ultimate secret – revealed!

Snoring like a chain saw, sawing logs . . . there are lots of funny names for it, but what causes people to snore, anyway? When you sleep, muscles in the back of your mouth and nose relax. That makes less room for air to get to your lungs and can create a loud vibration—a snore! Experts aren't quite sure why some of these sleepy snorts are louder than others, but factors such as age, weight, and allergies can all turn up the volume. And while snoring is usually harmless, superloud snores are sometimes a sign of a serious sleep disorder. And that's nothing to snooze at!

A
newborn
giraffe is the
height of a
**tall
man.**

Soaring up to 19 feet (6 m) tall, the giraffe is the tallest mammal on Earth. For more uplifting facts about tall things, turn to page 42.

this WAYUP

These **MULTILAYERED CLOUDS** are sometimes mistaken for UFOs because they appear to "hover" in one place for a long time.

RARE
HAT-SHAPED
CLOUDS

can be as tall as

2 EMPIRE STATE
BUILDINGS.

ultimate secret revealed!

What causes clouds to take on such a funny form?

Called lenticular clouds, or "lennies," these crazy clouds are usually created when high winds blow over rugged terrain such as mountain ranges. At Jotunheimen National Park in Norway, stable, strong gusts and moisture hit the high peaks. The wind forces the moisture upward, condensing into a cylindrical, saucer-like cloud. But there are no aliens on board this flying object—just a bunch of warm air.

AmAZiNG FLYING MaCHiNeS

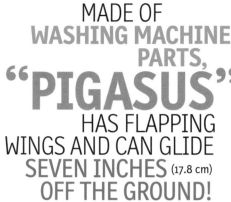

MADE OF WASHING MACHINE PARTS, **"PIGASUS"** HAS FLAPPING WINGS AND CAN GLIDE SEVEN INCHES (17.8 cm) OFF THE GROUND!

THE **FLYBOARD'S** POWERFUL **WATER JETS** LET YOU "FLY" **30 FEET** (9.1 m) ABOVE THE WATER!

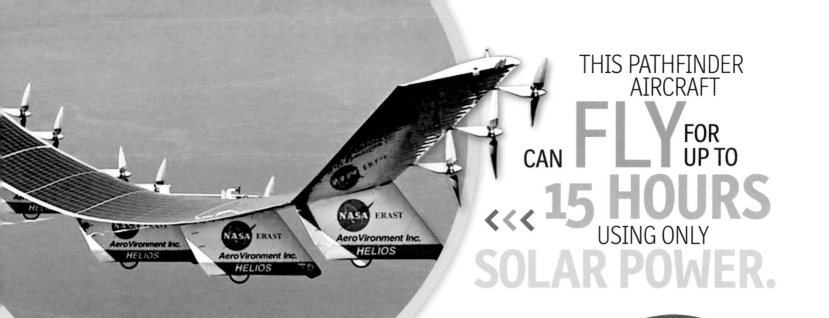

THIS PATHFINDER AIRCRAFT CAN **FLY** FOR UP TO <<< **15 HOURS** USING ONLY **SOLAR POWER.**

>>> THIS **HOVERCRAFT** CAN GLIDE OVER **LAND AND WATER** AND TRAVELS **FASTER** THAN A SPEEDING CAR.

<<< IT TAKES **16 ROTOR BLADES** TO LAUNCH THIS **ONE-SEAT MULTICOPTER** OFF THE GROUND.

>>> YOU CAN DRIVE THIS **STAR WARS—** INSPIRED **"HOVER BIKE"** WHILE SUSPENDED **15 FEET** IN THE AIR!
(4.6 m)

RHiNO Airlift

EXPERTS LOOPED WIDE STRAPS AROUND THE RHINOS' ANKLES, THEN ATTACHED THEM TO A LARGE HOOK DANGLING FROM THE HELICOPTER.

BLINDFOLDS WERE USED TO PREVENT THE ANIMALS FROM BECOMING SCARED IF THEY WERE TO WAKE UP.

THE FLIGHT ONLY TOOK TEN MINUTES. DRIVING THE RHINOS TO THEIR NEW HOME TOOK AN ADDITIONAL 21 HOURS.

On the Ground

A RHINO CALF becomes independent of its mother at about two and a half years old.

WALLOWING IN MUD helps protect a rhino from bugs and sunburn.

POACHERS OFTEN TARGET rhinos for their horns, which some cultures think have magical powers and medicinal properties. Rhino horns are also used for ornamental dagger handles.

RHINOS HAVE A strong sense of hearing and smell but don't see well.

Helicopters airlifted this rhino 3,200 FEET
(975 m)
in the air.

THE AIRLIFTED RHINOS WEIGHED AS MUCH AS 4,000 POUNDS (2,000 kg).

Fast FACTS

WHAT: Rhino Rescue

WHERE: Eastern Cape of South Africa

WHY FLY? To save this rhino and 18 others from poachers who want to kill the animals for their horns. An airlift is the gentlest way to get the rhinos out of their rugged habitat.

PRECIOUS CARGO: There are only about 4,880 black rhinos left in the wild. By moving them out of dangerous areas, humans hope they can help ensure the species' survival.

PLAYING IT SAFE: To protect the rhinos from distress, veterinarians put them to sleep before liftoff, then woke them up once they were secure in their new home in Limpopo Province, South Africa, more than 930 miles (1,500 km) away.

THE **FASTEST SPACECRAFT** EVER USED WOULD TAKE **70,000 YEARS** TO TRAVEL FROM EARTH TO THE NEAREST STAR OUTSIDE OUR SOLAR SYSTEM.

ALMOST EVERY **STAR** IN THE **MILKY**

DIFFERENT **PARTS** OF THE **SUN** **ROTATE** AT DIFFERENT **SPEEDS.**

BILLIONS OF YEARS AFTER SOME **STARS DIE,** THEY TURN INTO **GIANT DIAMONDS!**

STARS DON'T REALLY **TWINKLE,** THEY JUST LOOK THAT WAY FROM EARTH.

THE *FASTEST STARS* IN THE MILKY WAY CALLED **HYPERVELOCITY STARS** TRAVEL 530 MILES EVERY SECOND.

(853 km/s)

WAY HAS AT LEAST ONE **PLANET** ORBITING IT.

SIRIUS, THE BRIGHTEST STAR IN OUR NIGHT SKY, IS OFTEN MISTAKEN FOR A

UFO.

THE **STARS**

YOU SEE AT NIGHT LOOK SMALL BUT ARE ACTUALLY BIGGER THAN THE SUN.

THE LARGEST KNOWN **STAR** COULD BE

1,800 TIMES

LARGER THAN OUR SUN.

YOU CAN SEE **2,500 STARS** AT ONE TIME.

VHOEBE THE DOG CAN jump

seven feet in the AIR.
(2.1m)

(That's the height of some professional basketball players!)

→ This fit pooch runs on a treadmill, pulls weights, and sprints to prepare for her competitions.

→ With a running start, Vhoebe can leap more than 32 feet horizontally— (9.8 m) the length of a limousine!

→ Vhoebe travels around the United States to compete in jumping events, including "dock diving," in which she takes long leaps off docks into the water.

→ Vhoebe trains six days a week.

→ Even the best dog jumpers can't compete with cats, which can leap up to five times their own height in a single bound.

Hanging Out

∧
∧ **WHERE:**
∧ **23 feet** (7 m) **above**
Pfronten, Germany

WHAT'S UP?
Courageous **campers** climb ropes to access these **floating tents,** which hang from thick tree branches.

Love Is in the Air

〉〉〉

WHERE:
131 feet (40 m) **above**
Sint-Truiden, Belgium

WHAT'S UP?
This happy couple takes the **plunge**—literally—by **bungee jumping** off a platform after saying "I do."

UP
IN THE AIR

Pool With a View

WHERE:
650 feet (198 m)
above Singapore

WHAT'S UP?
This sky-high swimming spot is also **three times** the length of an **Olympic** swimming pool!

<<<

Flying High

WHERE:
24,262 feet (7,395 m) **above Somerset, England**

WHAT'S UP?
These **diners** are having a truly **elevated meal** while suspended from a hot-air balloon.

Tree House

WHERE:
15 feet (4.6 m) **above Qualicum Bay, British Columbia, Canada**

WHAT'S UP?
Visitors to Vancouver Island can sleep among the birds in one of these 11-foot (3.4-m)-wide **eco-friendly** tree houses.

WHERE:
692 feet (211 m) **above Dubai, United Arab Emirates**

WHAT'S UP?
This **tennis court,** temporarily built on a helipad atop a hotel, brings new meaning to the term **"air ball."**

Where's the Net?

Daring Dude!

Nock's death-defying feat didn't come without plenty of practice: The stuntman, who has been a tightrope-walker for more than four decades, also holds the record for the longest rope-walk over water!

HiGH-WiRE ACT

FastFACTS

WHO: Freddy Nock

WHAT: The longest and highest wire-walk without a balancing pole in history

WHERE: Zugspitze Mountain in Bavaria, Germany

HEIGHT: 9,721 feet (2,963 m)

TIME TO THE TOP: 1 hour, 20 minutes

LENGTH OF WALK: 3,280 feet (1,000 m)

THE WIRE IS ABOUT AS WIDE AS THREE PENNIES LINED UP.

THE WIRES ARE DESIGNED FOR CABLE CARS TO FERRY VISITORS UP AND DOWN THE MOUNTAIN.

THE STUNT WAS PART OF AN EFFORT TO RAISE MONEY FOR CHARITY.

NOCK GREW UP TRAVELING IN A CIRCUS AND STARTED WIRE-WALKING WHEN HE WAS ONLY FOUR YEARS OLD.

NOCK HIKED UP 1,142 FEET (348 m) ON THE WIRE TO REACH THE MOUNTAIN'S PEAK.

ALONG THE WAY, NOCK STOPPED TO FLASH A PEACE SIGN AND EVEN STOOD ON ONE FOOT!

TO KEEP HIS BALANCE, NOCK WALKS MOSTLY ON HIS TOES.

THIS **MAN** IS **walking** TO THE TOP OF GERMANY'S TALLEST MOUNTAIN on a two-inch-thick cable— (5-cm) WITH NO POLE OR SAFETY NET!

9 WEIRD FACTS ABOUT

The tallest **man** in history was **8 feet 11** inches tall. (2.7 m) His **head** nearly **hit** his living room ceiling.

SOME **HOT-AIR BALLOONS** ARE TALLER THAN THE **STATUE OF LIBERTY.**

A 45-FOOT-LONG, 800-POUND (363-kg) (13.7-m) **PAPER AIRPLANE** FLEW FOR ABOUT **TEN SECONDS** OVER AN ARIZONA DESERT.

BATOPHOBIA IS THE FEAR OF BEING NEAR TALL OBJECTS.

THE *FASTEST ELEVATOR,* TO BE COMPLETED IN 2014, IS EXPECTED TO TRAVEL **SIX STORIES** *IN ONE SECOND.*

RIDERS EXPERIENCE MOMENTS OF **WEIGHTLESSNESS** ON KINGDA KA, A 45-STORY-HIGH ROLLER COASTER IN NEW JERSEY, U.S.A.

THINGS THAT GO UP

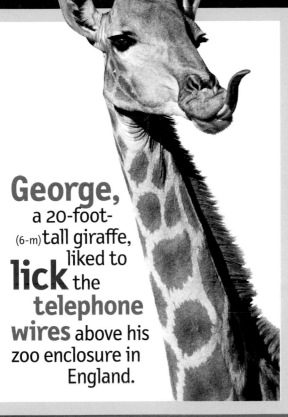

George, a 20-foot- (6-m) tall giraffe, liked to **lick** the **telephone wires** above his zoo enclosure in England.

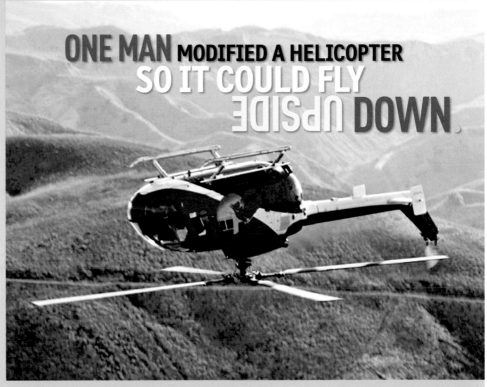

ONE MAN MODIFIED A HELICOPTER SO IT COULD FLY UPSIDE DOWN

THE HIGHEST- FLYING **BIRD** CAN SOAR ABOVE THE HIMALAYA, THE TALLEST MOUNTAIN RANGE ON EARTH.

Saturn's Secrets

THESE WACKY FACTS ABOUT THE **SIXTH PLANET** FROM THE SUN ARE DEFINITELY OTHERWORLDLY. WHO KNEW **SATURN** WAS SO STRANGE?

More than **763 EARTHS** would fit into Saturn.

SUMMER on Saturn lasts about **SEVEN EARTH** years.

Saturn is more than **745 MILLION MILES** (1.3 billion km) from Earth.

It's impossible to **WALK** on Saturn, because its surface is made mostly of **GAS.**

Each **RING** travels around Saturn at a different **SPEED.**

The **WINDS** on Saturn blow at about 1,118 miles an hour— (1,800 km/h) five times faster than the strongest HURRICANE winds on Earth!

If it were possible to WALK from Earth to Saturn, the JOURNEY would take more than 30,000 YEARS!

SATURN has 62 MOONS.

The average TEMPERATURE on Saturn is a FRIGID -288°F. (-178°C)

Saturn's RINGS are made mostly of ICE.

Saturn's RINGS STRETCH 46,000 MILES (74,030 km) into space.

It took one SPACECRAFT nearly SEVEN YEARS to get to Saturn.

Saturn is naturally BEIGE, but colored camera filters are used to make its colors BRIGHTER and details more visible.

A DAY on Saturn is 10 HOURS, 14 MINUTES long.

Saturn would FLOAT in WATER.

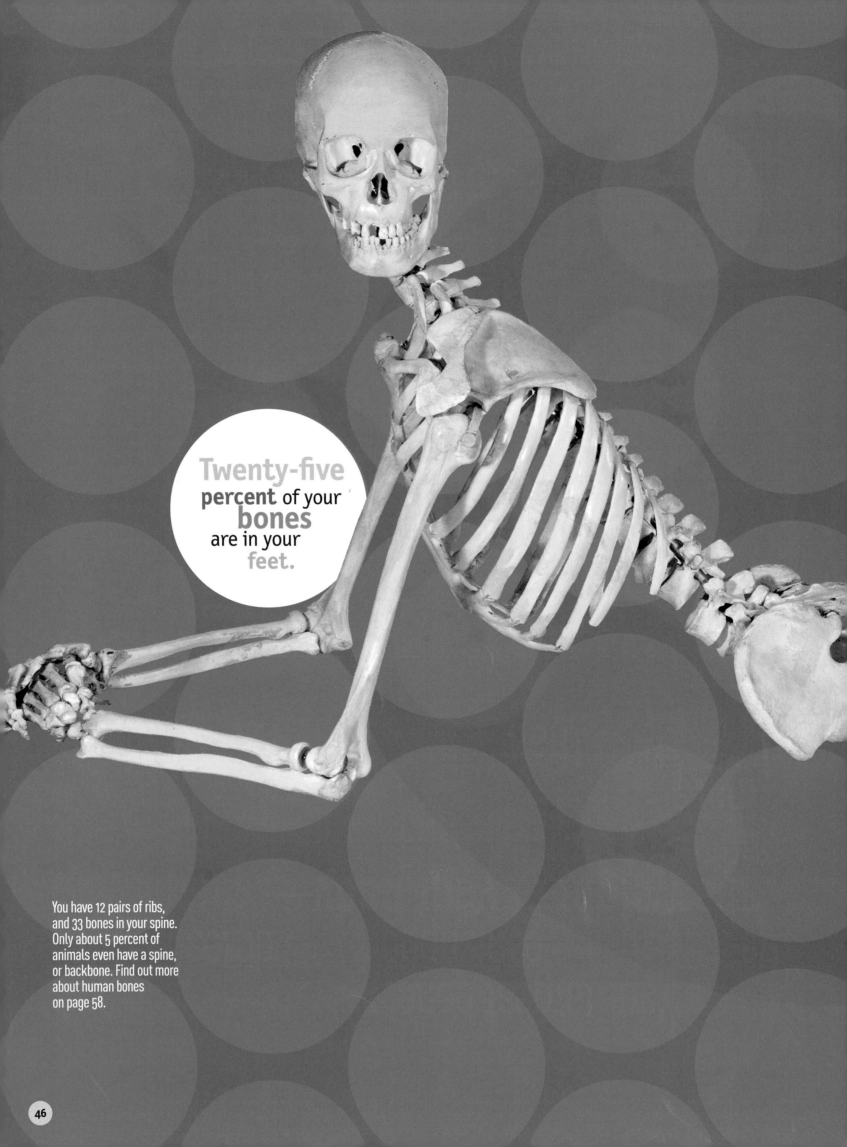

Twenty-five **percent** of your **bones** are in your **feet.**

You have 12 pairs of ribs, and 33 bones in your spine. Only about 5 percent of animals even have a spine, or backbone. Find out more about human bones on page 58.

CHAPTER 3

WHAT'S

YOUR NUMbER?

10 NEAT Nuggets ABOUT

Each **SQUARE INCH** (6.5 cm²) of **SKIN** on the **HUMAN BODY** contains about **32 MILLION** **BACTERIA.**

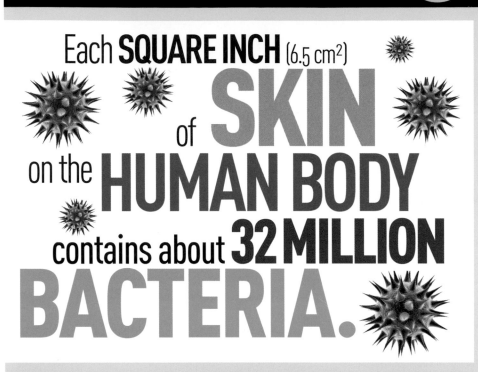

THE AVERAGE U.S. **TEENAGER** SENDS **60 TEXTS** A DAY.

THERE ARE ABOUT **2,000** **THUNDERSTORMS** **EARTH** ON AT ANY GIVEN MOMENT.

There are **239** **WAYS** to make **CHANGE** **FOR A DOLLAR.**

WORLDWIDE, PEOPLE SPEND **3 BILLION** HOURS A WEEK **PLAYING VIDEO GAMES.**

NUMBERS

7 BILLION HOT DOGS ARE **EATEN DURING THE SUMMER** IN THE UNITED STATES — **THAT'S ABOUT** **818** PER SECOND!

Kids in the U.S. will spend about **2,340 DAYS IN SCHOOL** from **KINDERGARTEN** through **HIGH SCHOOL.**

TAKING 1 BILLION STEPS IS LIKE WALKING AROUND THE GLOBE 19 TIMES.

IN CANADA, IF YOU **WIN A CONTEST, YOU NEED TO ANSWER A MATH QUESTION BEFORE YOU CAN CLAIM YOUR PRIZE.**

The **WORLD'S** MOST EXPENSIVE **NAIL POLISH,** which contains **267 CARATS** of **BLACK DIAMONDS,** sells for **$250,000 A BOTTLE.**

A BLUE WHALE'S TONGUE

IS ABOUT AS **HEAVY** AS . . .

2 Volkswagen Beetles

6 grand pianos

CAN WEiGH MORE THAN A FEMALE ELEPHANT.

10 snowmobiles

14 male African lions

Big, Bigger, Biggest!

LOUNGING LARGE!

THIS **6.6-TON** (5,987-kg) **DECK CHAIR** WAS INSTALLED ON A **BRITISH BEACH** TO **CELEBRATE** THE BEGINNING OF **SUMMER.**

>>>

AT **7** FEET **10** INCHES (2.4 m), THIS **HUGE** SNOWMAN **PEZ-DISPENSING MACHINE** IS **20** TIMES **BIGGER** THAN A NORMAL **PEZ DISPENSER!**

>>>

A PAIR OF **"A-MAZE-ING"** **18-ACRE** (7.3-ha) **CORN MAZES** WERE CREATED IN THE SHAPE OF **HARRY POTTER'S** FACE.

PLEASE DO NOT TOUCH

<<< 24,000 LEGO BRICKS WERE USED TO MAKE ONE **GIANT HANDBAG.** BUILDERS TOOK **20 DAYS** TO MAKE THIS NEARLY **220-POUND** (100-kg) **FASHION ACCESSORY.**

A **WRECKING BALL >>>** WAS USED TO LET LOOSE OVER **8,000** POUNDS (3,629 kg) OF **CANDY** HELD IN THIS SIX-STORY **PIÑATA.**

<<< THIS 150-POUND (68-kg) **DOG FOOD CAKE** HAS TASTY **INGREDIENTS** LIKE **BEEFSTEAK, DRIED LIVER,** AND **CHICKEN.**

TWINS ARE BORN IN ABOUT 1 IN 30 BIRTHS IN THE UNITED STATES.

1 IN 3 PEOPLE HAVE SLEEPWALKED AT LEAST ONCE.

THE ODDS OF GETTING STRUCK BY LIGHTNING IN YOUR LIFETIME: 1 IN 10,000.

YOU HAVE A 1 IN 1,000 CHANCE OF CATCHING A BASEBALL AT A NEW YORK YANKEES GAME.

THERE IS A COMPUTER PROGRAM THAT'S DESIGNED TO ANALYZE A SONG TO PREDICT THE CHANCES OF IT BECOMING A HIT.

WHEN 40 PEOPLE ARE IN A ROOM THERE IS A 90 PERCENT CHANCE 2 WILL HAVE THE SAME BIRTHDAY.

IN A STANDARD DECK OF CARDS, ONLY ONE OF THE FOUR KINGS HAS A MUSTACHE.

IN THE U.S., ONE OUT OF EVERY THREE PIZZAS SOLD IS TOPPED WITH PEPPERONI.

A PERSON IS OVER 100 TIMES MORE LIKELY TO DIE FROM A BEE STING THAN WIN A MEGAMILLIONS JACKPOT LOTTERY.

WILD OYSTERS YOU'D HAVE TO OPEN 12,000 TO EVEN HAVE A CHANCE OF FINDING A PEARL.

9 Totally WiLD

A **CROCODILE** GROWS up to **3,000** TEETH in its LIFETIME.

AN **ANTEATER'S** TONGUE IS **TWO FEET** (61 cm) LONG— that's about the LENGTH of a

TENNIS RACKET!

A **SQUID** HAS THREE HEARTS.

A **SLUG** HAS **FOUR** NOSES.

FACTS ABOUT ANiMALS

GiRAFFES HAVE **ZERO** VOCAL CORDS.

ABOUT **10 PERCENT** OF A **CAT'S** BONES ARE IN ITS TAIL.

A HUMMiNGBiRD'S WiNGS can beat up to **200 TiMES** a second.

THE WORLD'S **LEGGiEST** CREATURE —a **TYPE** of **MiLLiPEDE**— HAS **750** LEGS!

A **POLAR BEAR'S PAW** CAN BE **12 INCHES** (30 cm) **ACROSS**— THAT'S AS **WiDE** AS A **FRiSBEE.**

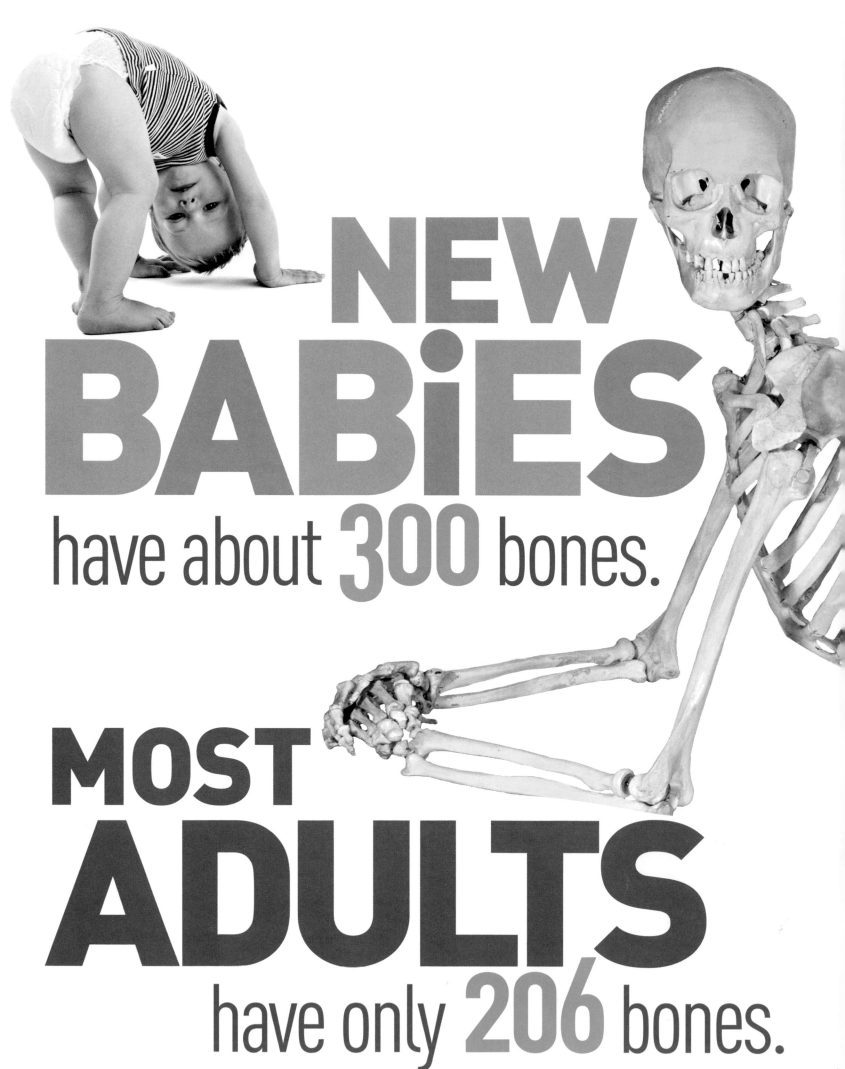

NEW BABiES

have about **300** bones.

MOST ADULTS

have only **206** bones.

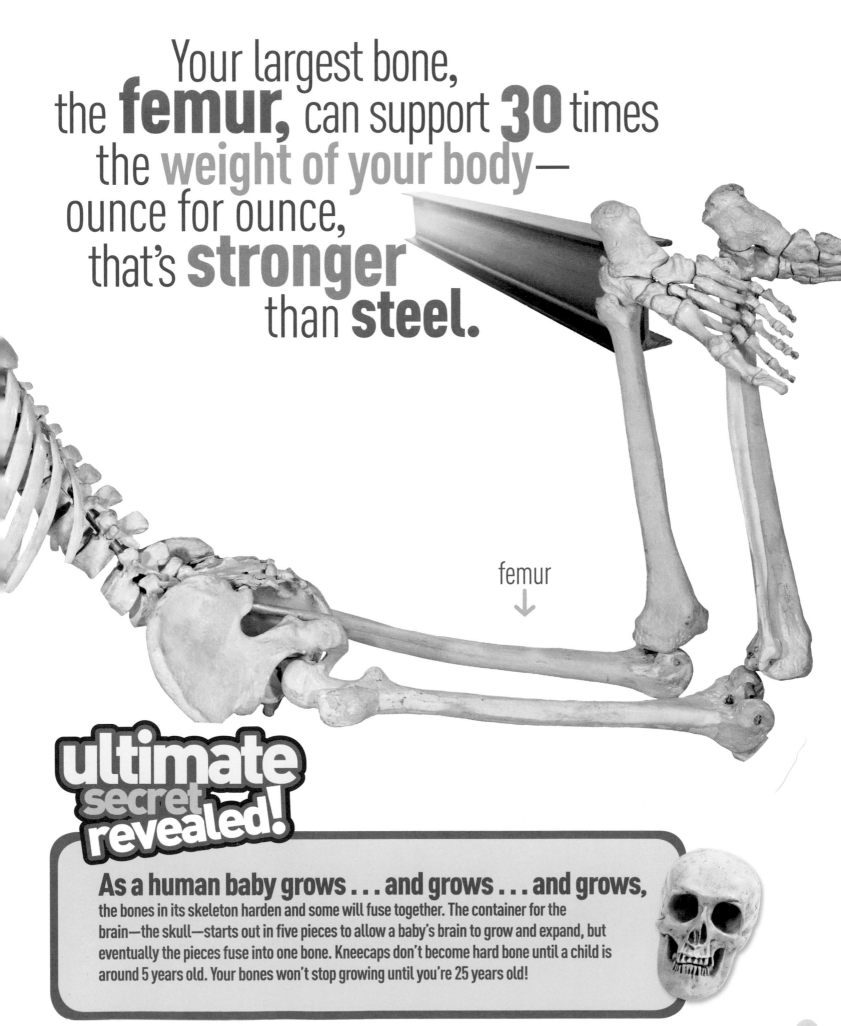

Your largest bone,
the **femur,** can support **30** times
the **weight of your body**—
ounce for ounce,
that's **stronger**
than **steel.**

femur
↓

ultimate secret revealed!

As a human baby grows . . . and grows . . . and grows, the bones in its skeleton harden and some will fuse together. The container for the brain—the skull—starts out in five pieces to allow a baby's brain to grow and expand, but eventually the pieces fuse into one bone. Kneecaps don't become hard bone until a child is around 5 years old! Your bones won't stop growing until you're 25 years old!

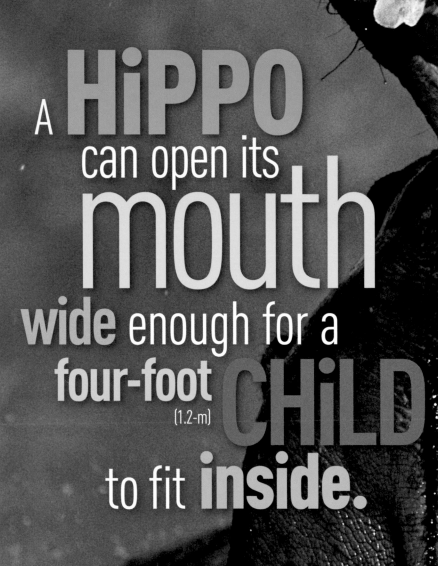

A **HiPPO** can open its **mouth** wide enough for a **four-foot** (1.2-m) **CHiLD** to fit **inside.**

What else could **fit inside** a **HIPPO'S MOUTH?**

2 Adélie penguins

4 prairie dogs

9 cardinals

14 northern leopard frogs

Small, Smaller, Smallest!

MILLY THE **CHIHUAHUA** IS **LESS THAN** **3 INCHES** (7.6 cm) **TALL**— **THAT'S SMALLER** THAN A **RAT!** >>>

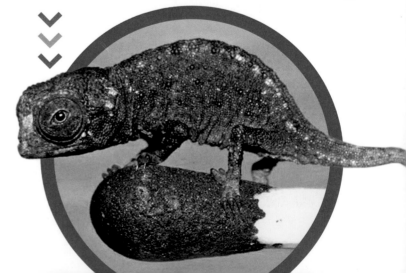

THIS **INCH**-(25-mm)**LONG** **CHAMELEON** FITS ON THE **HEAD** OF A **MATCHSTICK.**

^ ^ ^ THIS **TEENY TEA SET** WITH **TEACUPS** MEASURING LESS THAN **1/4 INCH** (6 mm) IS **DECORATED** IN **22-CARAT GOLD.**

THE **WORLD'S** SMALLEST <<< **SOLAR MOVIE THEATER,** **THE SOL CINEMA** IN WALES, U.K., SEATS ONLY **EIGHT ADULTS** AND **RUNS** ENTIRELY ON THE **POWER** OF THE **SUN!**

^^^ A **RESTAURANT** IN A **FIVE-STAR HOTEL** IN AUSTRIA **SEATS** ONLY **FOUR** PEOPLE!

THIS **PHONE BOOTH** IN ENGLAND WAS **TURNED INTO** ONE OF THE WORLD'S **TINIEST LIBRARIES.**

>>> THIS TINY **HARVEST MOUSE'S** BODY IS **TWO INCHES** (5 cm) **LONG** AND **WEIGHS** AS MUCH AS **A QUARTER.**

There are 1.4 billion insects for every human on Earth.

enter the SWARM

FastFACTS

If you gathered up every single termite, they would weigh more than all the humans on Earth!

There are more than 360,000 kinds of beetles—that's more than all the planet's plant species.

The oldest insect fossil is 410 million years old.

There are 900,000 known insect species, but not all of them have scientific names yet.

It takes scientists a year to name 4,400 new species of insects. It would take scientists 1,364 years to name and describe the more than 6 million insect species believed to exist on Earth.

Now known as Jetman, inventor Yves Rossy has also been nicknamed Rocketman, Airman, and even Fusionman for his solo adventures in flight. Find out more about Jetman's adventures on page 72.

Daredevil pilot **Jetman** once **skysurfed** from the top of a **hot-air balloon.**

CHAPTER 4

OVER THE TOP

A BRITISH **MAN** COLLECTED **1,600** GnOMES AND FILLED HIS COTTAGE & GARDEN WITH them.

Dressed-Up Dogs!

^^^ THIS **PAINTED PUP** WAS **DECORATED** LIKE A **TIGER** FOR A CELEBRATION OF A **NEW PET PARK** IN **CHINA.**

JOHNNY DEPP AS ❯ CAPTAIN JACK SPARROW

IT CAN ❯❯❯ TAKE UP TO **SIX MONTHS** TO GROW A **DOG'S HAIR** LONG ENOUGH TO **STYLE** LIKE THIS **PUFFY PANDA** PUP'S.

SEPARATED ^^ AT **BIRTH?** THIS **GROOMED SWASHBUCKLER** LOOKS JUST LIKE **JACK SPARROW** FROM *PIRATES OF THE CARIBBEAN.*

CINDY THE DOG WAS **STYLED** TO LOOK LIKE A **MINI CAMEL.** >>>

<<< CREATIVE GROOMERS **TREAT** THIS **DOG** LIKE A **QUEEN** BY **DRESSING HER UP** AS ONE!

ONE PHOTOGRAPHER **TRAVELS** THOUSANDS OF MILES EVERY YEAR TO **SNAP PICTURES** AT CREATIVE GROOMING DOG SHOWS. **"SAY CHEESE!"** **POODLE-PEACOCK.** >>>

< ANIMAL FROM *THE MUPPET SHOW*

<<< THIS **WEST HIGHLAND TERRIER** WAS **GROOMED** TO LOOK LIKE **ANIMAL** FROM *THE MUPPET SHOW.*

FLYING on the Wing

FastFACTS

WHO: Yves Rossy

WHAT: Swiss pilot

WHERE: Rio de Janeiro, Brazil

WHEN: May 2, 2012

WHY: For the thrill of flight

JETMAN'S AVERAGE FLIGHT TIME IS TEN MINUTES.

JETMAN IS THE FIRST MAN EVER TO FLY WITH A JET-PROPELLED WING.

IT TOOK MORE THAN TEN YEARS AND MORE THAN 15 MODELS TO MAKE A SUCCESSFUL JET WING.

THE WING CAN CLIMB AT A RATE OF 1,083 FEET (330 m) PER MINUTE.

JETMAN CARRIES ALMOST EIGHT GALLONS (30 L) OF FUEL.

A pilot nicknamed **JETMAN** used a *jet-propelled wing* to go **124 miles an hour** (200 km/h) around Rio de Janeiro, Brazil.

THIS STATUE, CALLED "CHRIST THE REDEEMER," IS ONE OF THE NEW SEVEN WONDERS OF THE WORLD.

RIO IS ALSO KNOWN AS *CIDADE MARAVILHOSA* — OR "THE MARVELOUS CITY."

THE 125-FOOT (38 m) STATUE SITS ON TOP OF CORCOVADO MOUNTAIN.

JETMAN has also been spotted over …

the Grand Canyon

Abu Dhabi, capital of the United Arab Emirates

the English Channel

the Swiss Alps

air shows

8 Wacky FACTS ABOUT

57 pounds (26 kg) OF **BEES** **SWARMED** ON THE **WINNER'S SKIN** IN A "**bee-attracting**" **CONTEST** IN **China.**

At the World **Pea-Shooting** Championship, some **competitors** use **laser-guided shooters** to **blow PEAS** at a target **36 feet** (11 m) **away.**

In **CHESSBOXiNG,** PLAYERS switch BETWEEN **boxing** and **chess** EVERY FEW MINUTES.

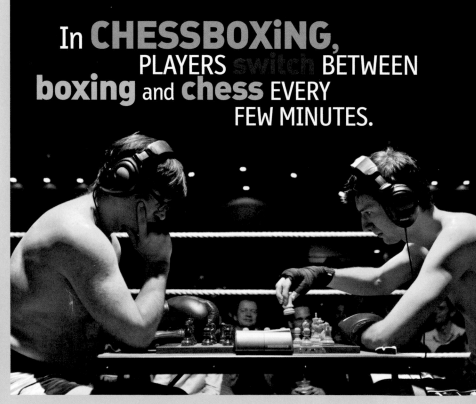

The **world** WORM-CHARMiNG CHAMPIONS took a **HALF HOUR** to "**charm**" **567** WORMS into **SLiTHERING** OUT OF THE EARTH.

CRAZY Contests

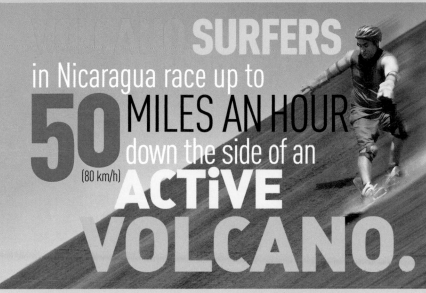

VOLCANO SURFERS in Nicaragua race up to **50** MILES AN HOUR (80 km/h) down the side of an **ACTIVE VOLCANO.**

RUNNERS BRAVE **SNOW** SQUALLS and WIND CHILLS of **-4°F** (-20°C) TO COMPLETE A **MARATHON** IN **ANTARCTICA.**

At the **GRAND NATIONAL** Calling Championships, people compete to see whose **GOBBLE SOUNDS** the most like a **TURKEY.**

A MAN GULPED DOWN **72** CUPCAKES IN **6** MINUTES AT AN EATING COMPETITION— SETTING A NEW RECORD!

There are more than **100 million** pieces of **junk** **ORBITING** Earth.

Millions of the **pieces are tiny,** but most **space junk** can **ZIP** around **Earth's orbit** at **17,000 miles an hour** (27,000 km/h)!

ultimate secret revealed!

Earth needs some galactic garbage control.
There are about 21,000 pieces of space junk greater than 3.9 inches (10 cm)—mostly exploded or old satellites, pieces of discarded rockets, and other garbage caused by space exploration. One astronaut's glove has been whizzing around space since he lost it in 1965! All this junk collides with other space objects—creating even more pieces of junk. Will it ever be cleaned? Switzerland announced development of a satellite called CleanSpace One to collect the trash. Wall·E would be proud!

St. Elmo's Fire

It's not actually fire at all—it's a gas called plasma. Metallic or pointy objects often become supercharged during thunderstorms. When the charges are high enough, the air around the object also becomes charged, or ionized. The nitrogen and oxygen in the air cause the glow to be blue or violet, and the St. Elmo's light can continue for several minutes.

>>>

Weird Weather

TIRED OF SUN, CLOUDS, AND ALL THE USUAL STUFF WHEN YOU PEEK OUT YOUR WINDOW? **CHECK OUT** THESE EXCITING WEATHER CONDITIONS THAT WILL **BLOW YOU AWAY!**

Waterspout

These water funnels form in two ways: when a tornado moves over water, or when wind is light but cumulus clouds are developing. The second kind starts swirling at the surface of the water and moves upward. If these reach land, they'll fall apart rather quickly—and get you wet!

<<<

<<< Haboob

A haboob is a giant desert dust storm. The thick blanket of dust can swallow up a city, knock over power lines, and cause traffic accidents because of reduced visibility. Cover your mouth and nose and run for cover if a haboob comes your way.

<<< Double Rainbow

Light reflecting inside water droplets causes one rainbow, but it's actually possible for light to be reflected more than once inside a raindrop. The rare secondary rainbow is formed above the first and is usually fainter—and the colors are seen in the reverse order. Intense!

Red Sprite

Red sprites are still a bit mysterious to scientists. They happen in the upper atmosphere, miles above thunderstorms that are ending. After much of the electric charge is removed from a storm through lightning strikes, these glowing streamers may appear. Red sprites are rarely seen from Earth.
>>>

>>> Sky Punch

Sometimes you'll see a stretch of clouds across the sky, and then a few minutes later—*BAM!*—there's a hole punched right through it! This phenomenon is caused when supercooled clouds lay like a blanket across the sky and an airplane flies through the cloud layer. The broken cloud section actually falls as snow!

This **creature** can **survive** for more than **100 years** without **water.**

495 times actual size

They're **known as** **water bears** or **moss piglets** — and you can **find them** in **your** **backyard!**

ultimate **secret** **revealed!**

Its proper name is the tardigrade, and it's one of the world's toughest creatures. It lives in soil, on lichens and mosses, and in all kinds of fresh- and saltwater environments. You'll find them at the top of the Himalaya, at the bottom of the sea, and from the Equator to the Poles. But you have to look extremely closely. Most are about .04 inch (1 mm). They can survive freezing conditions close to -459°F (-273°C), and even X-ray exposure more than 1,000 times greater than the amount that would kill a human. What's the water bear's secret? When the going gets tough, it curls up and switches off its metabolism, going into an extreme state of hibernation, called cryptobiosis. Then it wakes when things are looking up. Lucky bear!

Extremely Expensive Stuff

<<< THIS **BARBIE** AND HER **DIAMOND NECKLACE** SOLD AT AN **AUCTION** FOR **$302,500**—ALL **DONATED** TO A **CANCER RESEARCH** GROUP.

A CHINESE MAN BOUGHT A >>> **RED TIBETAN MASTIFF** NAMED **HONG DONG,** WHOSE NAME MEANS **"BIG SPLASH,"** FOR **$1.5 MILLION.**

<<< **500 DIAMONDS** ENCRUST THIS **24-CARAT GOLD iPHONE 4S,** WHICH SOLD FOR AROUND **$8 MILLION.**

WHAT COMES WITH A **$1 MILLION**
<<< GOLD-PLATED VACUUM?
A **LIFETIME WARRANTY,**
FREE **SHIPPING,** AN **ENGRAVING,**
AND A **CLEAN FLOOR.**

THIS **>>>**
GOLD-PLATED **SUV**
HAS **BULLETPROOF**
WINDOWS AND
EIGHT CAMERAS
ON THE OUTSIDE—PLUS A
PRICE TAG OF MORE
THAN A **HALF-MILLION**
DOLLARS.

<<<
THIS **$25,000**
CHOCOLATE SUNDAE
COMES WITH
EDIBLE GOLD FLAKES,
A **SOUVENIR** GOLD AND
DIAMOND BRACELET,
AND AN **18-CARAT**
GOLD SPOON.

83

→ Iron Man, a Marvel Comics superhero, wears an armored suit that gives him superpowers.

How about a movie deal for me?

→ Comic book fan Mark Pearson's replica took him 14 months to make, but it doesn't fly.

→ There are real-life robot suits out there, and they can increase the wearer's strength to 17 times above normal.

IRON MAN IN THE 2008 BLOCKBUSTER MOVIE

This NEAR-PERFECT REPLICA of Iron Man's suit is actually made of cardboard and fiberglass.

Zookeepers sometimes apply **sunscreen** to albino animals' skin to prevent **sunburn.**

Nala is one of only a few known albino kangaroos in the world. Because of their astonishing all-white appearance, albino animals are also known as "ghosts of nature." Check out some more wild creatures on page 100.

only IT'S NATURAL

Otter and Kittens

WHERE THEY LIVE:
Somerset, England, U.K.

WHY THEY'RE WACKY:
This cuddly crew **bonded** shortly after birth, when zookeepers paired the orphaned otter with this litter of kittens. They did almost **everything together** until the otter was ready to return to the wild.

Dog and Deer

WHERE THEY LIVE:
Vancouver Island, British Columbia, Canada

WHY THEY'RE WACKY:
This Great Dane and black-tailed deer **stroll** in the woods together and **play** outside for hours.

Bush Baby and Baboon

WHERE THEY LIVE:
Nairobi, Kenya

WHY THEY'RE WACKY:
This young baboon takes this **orphaned bush baby** wherever she goes, carrying her around and even **sharing** her milk out of the same bowl.

WaCKy ANIMAL FRiENDSHiPS

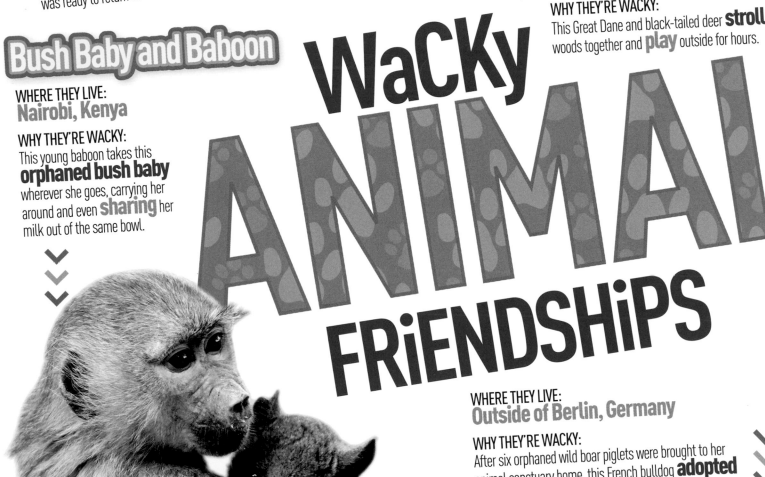

WHERE THEY LIVE:
Outside of Berlin, Germany

WHY THEY'RE WACKY:
After six orphaned wild boar piglets were brought to her animal sanctuary home, this French bulldog **adopted** them as her own, **snuggling** them to keep them warm.

Bulldog and Piglets

Dolphin and Seal

WHERE THEY LIVE:
Coffs Harbour,
New South Wales, Australia

WHY THEY'RE WACKY:
These unlikely pals would be rivals in the wild, but in the Dolphin Marine Magic park they're **inseparable,** loving to play, swim, and even perform **"kisses."**

Iguana and Cat

WHERE THEY LIVE:
Brooklyn, New York, U.S.A.

WHY THEY'RE WACKY:
You wouldn't think a cat and an iguana would have anything in common, but this **pair loves** lounging around and taking naps together.

Cheetah and Dog

WHERE THEY LIVE:
Tampa, Florida, U.S.A.

WHY THEY'RE WACKY:
Raised together at an animal park, this yellow lab and cheetah are **best buds,** spending their days chasing each other around just for fun!

SUPeR-TrEES

AT NIGHT THE TREES' LIGHTS CHANGE COLORS TO THE BEAT OF MUSIC PIPED IN THROUGHOUT THE PARK.

THE TREES SERVE AS "VERTICAL GARDENS" WITH MORE THAN 200 SPECIES OF PLANTS AND FLOWERS GROWING FROM THEIR TRUNKS.

FastFACTS

NAME: Supertree Grove

WHAT: Eighteen giant artificial trees powered by solar panels at the tops of their trunks

WHERE: Marina Bay, Singapore

HEIGHT: Some of these Supertrees are taller than New York City's Statue of Liberty!

COST: The trees and the surrounding park cost more than $1 billion to build.

Water WATER Everywhere

These eco-friendly trees catch rain that's used to fill the park's fountains and water the plants.

VISITORS CAN WALK FROM TREE TO TREE VIA A SKY BRIDGE 72 FEET (22 m) ABOVE THE GROUND.

THERE'S A RESTAURANT AT THE TOP OF THE TALLEST TREE.

THE TREES' TRUNKS, MADE OF STEEL AND CONCRETE, WEIGH HUNDREDS OF TONS EACH.

THESE AMAZING man-made trees SOAR up to 164 feet high— (50 m) as TALL as a 16-story BUILDING!

SOME people SMELL COLORS and TASTE SHAPES.

The **BODY** can detect taste in .0015 SECONDS— that's faster than the **BLINK** of an eye.

How can the senses get so mixed up?

About 1 in 2,000 people has a rare condition called synesthesia. The input of one sense causes the experience of another sense because messages to and from the brain get mixed up. The condition might cause a person to see a rich blue color when they eat steak. The sound of a violin might be detected as a tickle on the face instead of just a sound. These sensory experiences are automatic and can't be controlled. The most common form of synesthesia is "color hearing," in which people hear sounds as colors.

What a Blast!

HANG ON TIGHT, BECAUSE THESE EXPLOSIVE FACTS ABOUT VOLCANOES WILL BLOW YOUR MIND!

About **75%** of the world's volcanoes are located in a **RING** around the Pacific Ocean called the **RING OF FIRE**.

LAVA can be **HOT** as as **2200°F.** (1200°C)

ERUPTIONS can be **1,600 TIMES** stronger than an atomic blast.

This volcano, called **PITON DE LA FOURNAISE,** is located on Reunion Island in the Indian Ocean.

Its name means **"PEAK OF THE FURNACE,"** in French.

Eruptions can BLAST ROCK at 650 MILES an hour. (1,000 km/h)

MOST of the world's volcanoes are UNDER the ocean.

Some volcanic ROCK can FLOAT on water.

One of the world's most ACTIVE volcanoes, Piton de la Fournaise, has erupted over 150 times in the past 300 YEARS.

Volcanoes give off POISONOUS GASES.

This volcano is more than HALF A MILLION years old.

The strongest ERUPTIONS can temporarily change the world's CLIMATE.

The coolest lava GLOWS RED; the hottest lava glows ORANGE AND YELLOW.

Some volcanoes provide enough ENERGY to heat ENTIRE CITIES.

One in ten people on Earth lives CLOSE enough to a volcano to be in a DANGER ZONE.

The word "VOLCANO" comes from the name of the Roman god of fire, VULCAN.

95

9 WILD FACTS ABOUT

A **CAT** IN RUSSIA **BARKS** LIKE A **DOG.**

LEATHERBACK TURTLES CAN **swim** IN A STRAIGHT LINE FOR THOUSANDS OF miles. (km)

The **brains** of some small spiders **spill** over into their **legs.**

THERE'S A VIRUS THAT MAKES SNAKES TWIST THEMSELVES INTO KNOTS.

OLD TERMITES WILL EXPLODE TO PROTECT THEIR NESTS.

ANIMAL ODDITIES

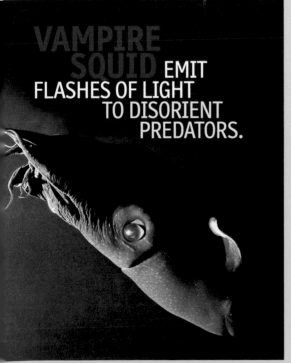

RATS can **POP** their **EYES** out of their **SOCKETS.**

AN **ELEPHANT LEARNED TO IMITATE** THE WORDS **"HELLO"** AND **"SIT DOWN" IN KOREAN.**

VAMPIRE SQUID EMIT FLASHES OF LIGHT TO DISORIENT PREDATORS.

CHINESE SOFT-SHELLED **turtles** URINATE THROUGH THEIR MOUTHS.

POWERS OF NATURE

Check out how these forces of nature measure up in our everyday lives.

CATEGORY 5 HURRICANE

HOW FAST IS IT?
Wind speeds can reach **157 MILES AN HOUR** (253 km/h) or faster.

THAT'S ALMOST AS SPEEDY AS A NASCAR race car.

LIGHTNING BOLT

HOW HOT IS IT?
The air around a lightning bolt can be as hot as **54,000°F** (30,000°C).

THAT'S FIVE TIMES HOTTER THAN THE SURFACE of the sun.

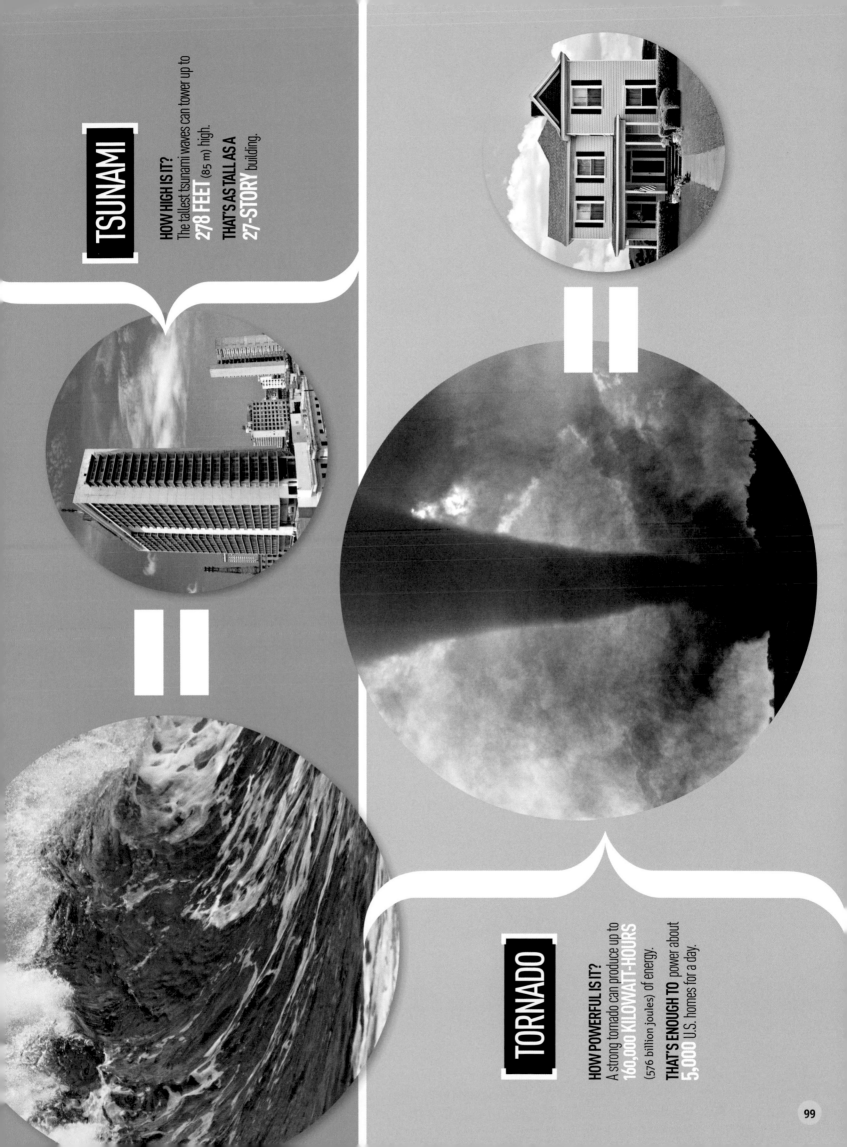

TSUNAMI

HOW HIGH IS IT?
The tallest tsunami waves can tower up to **278 FEET** (85 m) high.

THAT'S AS TALL AS A 27-STORY building.

TORNADO

HOW POWERFUL IS IT?
A strong tornado can produce up to **160,000 KILOWATT-HOURS** (576 billion joules) of energy.

THAT'S ENOUGH TO power about **5,000** U.S. homes for a day.

Dumbo Octopus

WHERE IT LIVES:
On the ocean floor, up to 15,750 feet (4,800 m) below sea level

WHY IT'S FREAKY:
This **deep-sea creature** gets its name from tiny fins at the top of its body. When the octopus flaps its fins to swim, it looks like **Dumbo** the flying elephant!

Albino Kangaroo

WHERE IT LIVES:
At a zoo in Germany

WHY IT'S FREAKY:
This rare 'roo—born **without pigment** (or color) in its skin, eyes, and fur—probably would not survive long in the wild without a **kangaroo's** usual brown camouflage.

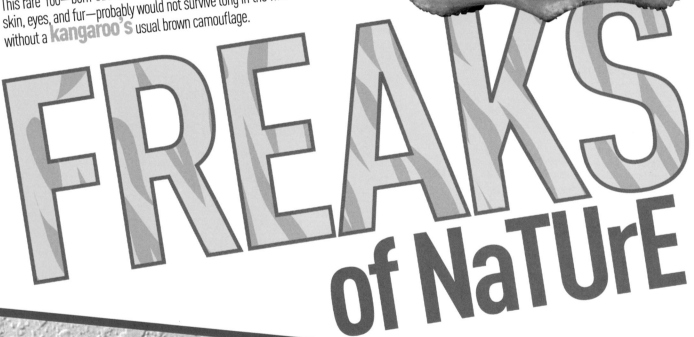

FREAKS of NaTUrE

Two-Faced Feline

WHERE IT LIVES:
Florida, U.S.A.

WHY IT'S FREAKY:
Because the color on this kitty's face is **split** straight down the middle, experts think this **crazy-looking** cat may have different DNA on each side of her body.

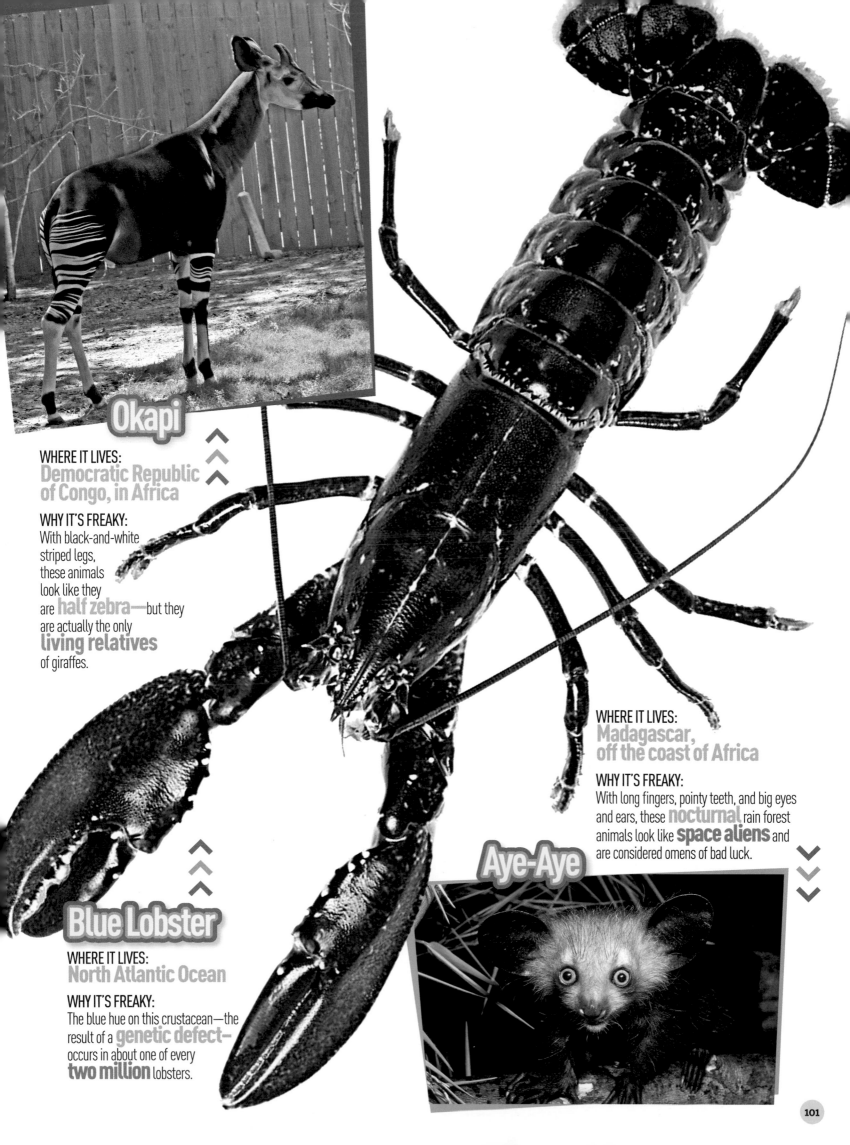

Okapi

WHERE IT LIVES:
Democratic Republic of Congo, in Africa

WHY IT'S FREAKY:
With black-and-white striped legs, these animals look like they are **half zebra**—but they are actually the only **living relatives** of giraffes.

Blue Lobster

WHERE IT LIVES:
North Atlantic Ocean

WHY IT'S FREAKY:
The blue hue on this crustacean—the result of a **genetic defect**—occurs in about one of every **two million** lobsters.

WHERE IT LIVES:
Madagascar, off the coast of Africa

WHY IT'S FREAKY:
With long fingers, pointy teeth, and big eyes and ears, these **nocturnal** rain forest animals look like **space aliens** and are considered omens of bad luck.

Aye-Aye

Scientists are watching how **ANT COLONIES** MOVE in hopes of making the INTERNET FASTER.

A **SCIENTIST** came up with the IDEA for Velcro when he saw burrs stuck to a **DOG'S FUR.**

ultimate secret revealed!

How can studying nature help us make a more high-tech world?

What could ants teach us about the Internet? While watching harvester ants search for food, scientists noticed that if the ants returned with food quickly, the colony knew that food was nearby. If the ants took a long time to come back, food was farther away. This system is similar to the one used to test the Internet's bandwidth.

Studying ants may help scientists make the Internet even faster in the future. Studying nature for solutions to high-tech problems is called biomimicry, and the concept has been around for a long time. In 1941, a Swiss inventor noticed the way sharp plant burrs stuck to his dog's soft fur, giving him the idea for Velcro. Today, engineers study locust swarms and apply their anti-collision system to cars. Sounds like scientists are really getting back to nature!

THERE IS THREE TIMES MORE

OXYGEN

IN THE AIR AT SEA LEVEL THAN AT THE TOP OF EVEREST.

A COUPLE GOT MARRIED AT THE TOP OF EVEREST IN 2005.

THE YOUNGEST PERSON TO SUMMIT EVEREST WAS 13 YEARS OLD.

IF EVEREST WERE DROPPED INTO THE DEEPEST PART OF THE OCEAN, ITS

PEAK

WOULD BE MORE THAN A

MILE
(1.6 km)

UNDERWATER.

TWO MEN CLIMBED EVEREST, PARAGLIDED DOWN, AND THEN KAYAKED TO THE INDIAN OCEAN.

THE ROCKS

ON EVEREST, IT CAN TAKE AS LITTLE AS **FIVE MINUTES** FOR YOUR **FACE** TO GET **FROSTBITTEN.**

THE FIRST MEN TO SUMMIT **EVEREST** BURIED **COOKIES AND CANDY** IN THE **SNOW** AS AN OFFERING TO BUDDHIST GODS.

THE HIGHEST WIND SPEED ON THE SUMMIT IS **175 MPH** (282 km/h) —THAT'S MORE POWERFUL THAN A CATEGORY 5 HURRICANE.

AT **29,035 FEET** (8,850 m) EVEREST IS TALLER THAN 29 EIFFEL TOWERS STACKED UP.

THAT MAKE UP **EVEREST** WERE ONCE ON THE **SEAFLOOR.**

An **adult rat** can fit through a **hole** as small as a quarter.

A rat's front teeth grow five inches (12.7 cm) per year, so rats are always gnawing on things to file down their teeth. Find out how this pesky animal got along with folks in the Middle Ages on page 116.

CHAPTER 6

THAt'S CREEPY!

Fried Centipede

WHAT IT IS: Centipede on a STICK

WHY IT'S SCARY: If you're at a night STREET MARKET in Beijing, China, you might be more likely to find a fried centipede on a stick than a CORN DOG.

<<<

ScaryFOOD

Candy Collage

WHAT IT IS: Halloween candy MOSAIC

WHY IT'S SCARY: These candies form the PORTRAIT of one of Halloween's freakiest characters—FRANKENSTEIN!

Dragon Fruit

WHAT IT IS: Pitaya or pitahaya—pink BULB with sweet pulp and black seeds

WHY IT'S SCARY: Not only is this CACTUS fruit wacky-looking, but its flower only blooms at NIGHT during a full moon!

Love Bug Salad

- **WHAT IT IS:** **DELICACY** at a fine London, England, restaurant

- **WHY IT'S SCARY:** This spinach and arugula **SALAD** is served with **LOCUSTS AND CRICKETS** pan-fried with chili and garlic.

Killer Bee Larvae

- **WHAT IT IS:** Bug babies on **SUSHI**

- **WHY IT'S SCARY:** Bug-eating **PARTIES** are all the rage in Tokyo, Japan. **SNACK** on this party dish of killer bee larvae served on sushi.

Looking good for 40 . . .

Devil Skull Cake

WHAT IT IS: **BIRTHDAY** cake

WHY IT'S SCARY: **DIG** into this birthday cake . . . if you dare. It could either be a **NIGHTMARE,** or devilishly delicious.

Chocolate Leech

WHAT IT IS: **BLOOD-SUCKING** leech . . . in candy form!

WHY IT'S SCARY: These realistic creepy crawly candies are **CAST** in chocolate and **PAINTED** in colored cocoa butter.

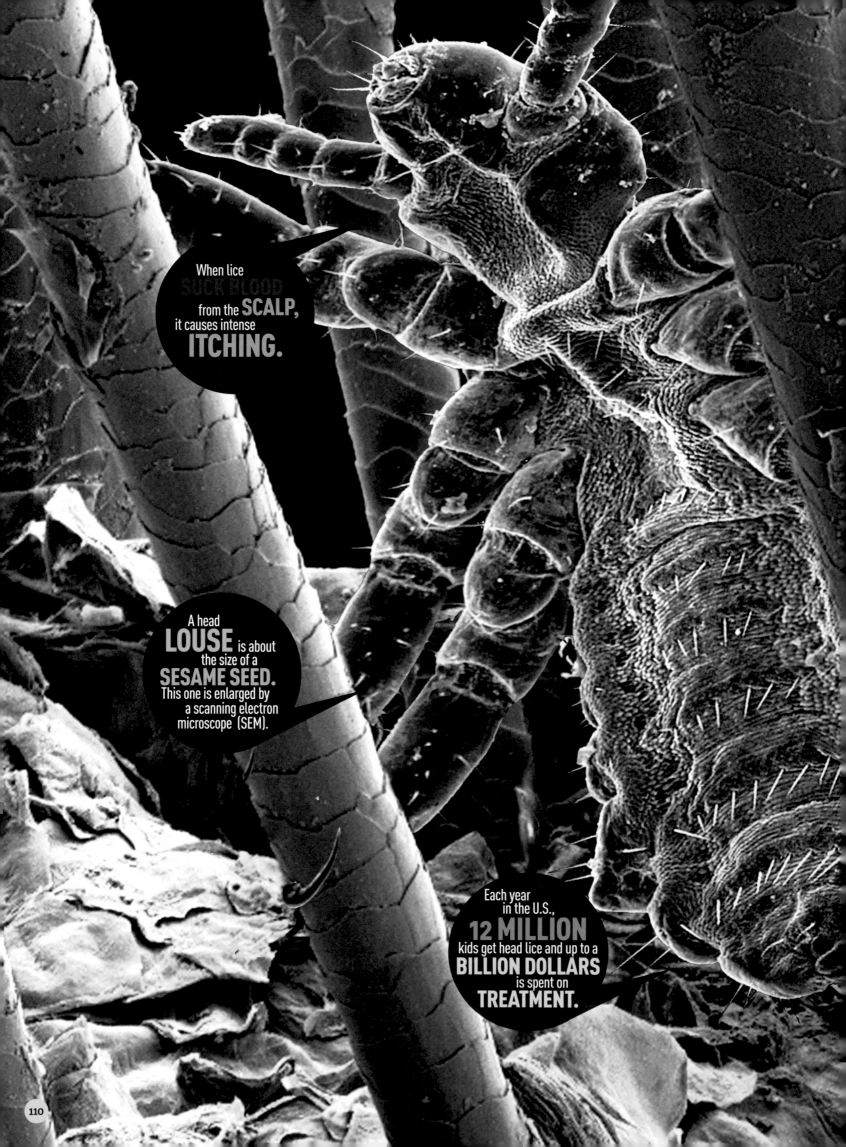

When lice
SUCK BLOOD
from the SCALP,
it causes intense
ITCHING.

A head
LOUSE is about
the size of a
SESAME SEED.
This one is enlarged by
a scanning electron
microscope (SEM).

Each year
in the U.S.,
12 MILLION
kids get head lice and up to a
BILLION DOLLARS
is spent on
TREATMENT.

LICE **EGGS** are called **NITS.**

FEELING ITCHY?

THIS **CREATURE** LIVES CLOSE TO THE **HUMAN** SCALP, SUCKING BLOOD AND LAYING EGGS IN YOUR HAIR.

FiSH SCALES
ARE AN INGREDIENT IN SOME
LiPSTiCKS.

COSMETICS CAN ALSO CONTAIN:
RED FOOD COLORING MADE FROM **CRUSHED BUGS** (LIPSTICK),
FOSSILIZED REMAINS OF A KIND OF ALGAE (DEODORANT, NATURAL TOOTHPASTE),
AND EVEN PLASTIC (HAIRSPRAY).

Why are cosmetics made with such weird ingredients?

Even ancient cultures from around the world experimented with beauty products. And we continue to do so today! The silvery substance that makes fish look shimmery is the same stuff used in some shiny lipsticks. Called pearl essence, it's found in many types of fish scales. Herring scales are most commonly used. The ingredient is sometimes used in nail polish, ceramics, and paints that have a shimmery look. Herring scales, along with algae, come from animals and can be listed as "natural ingredients."

Freaky
PHOBIAS

FEAR INCREASES YOUR HEART RATE BY AS MUCH AS **20** BEATS PER MINUTE.

CHRONOMENTROPHOBIA
Fear of clocks

COULROPHOBIA
Fear of clowns

CYBERPHOBIA
Fear of computers

HOMICHLOPHOBIA
Fear of fog

SAMHAINOPHOBIA
Fear of Halloween

CATOPTROPHOBIA
Fear of mirrors

PAPYROPHOBIA
Fear of paper

MICROPHOBIA
Fear of small things

CHIONOPHOBIA
Fear of snow

EPHEBIPHOBIA
Fear of teenagers

10 Menacing Facts ABOUT THE

FOOD & DRINK WOULDN'T LAST FOREVER DURING A **CASTLE SIEGE.** EVENTUALLY KNIGHTS WOULD RESORT TO EATING ANYTHING LEFT: **RATS, HORSES, BUGS,** EVEN **GRASS.**

MUMMIFIED HUMAN REMAINS **GROUND** INTO A **POULTICE, POTION, OR OTHER SOLUTION** **CURE** WERE THOUGHT TO ALMOST EVERY AILMENT.

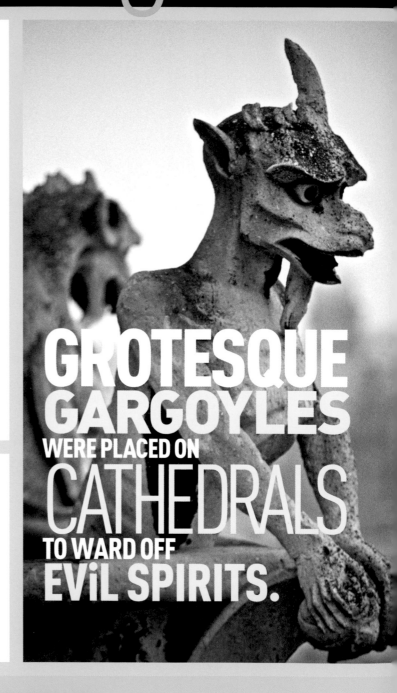

GROTESQUE GARGOYLES **WERE PLACED ON** CATHEDRALS **TO WARD OFF** EVIL SPIRITS.

BESIEGERS SOMETIMES *CATAPULTED* BODIES, SEWAGE—EVEN **SEVERED** HEADS— **INTO CASTLES TO SPREAD DISEASE AND TERROR.**

MIDDLE AGES

A **POPULAR** DISH AMONG **ROYALTY** WAS **PIE** MADE WITH **LAMPREY—** A **SLIMY**, EEL-LIKE **FISH.**

MANY **PEOPLE** BELIEVED IN **VAMPIRES** AND THOUGHT THEY WERE TO BLAME FOR **PLAGUES.**

PEOPLE THOUGHT **CAVITIES** WERE CAUSED BY **WORMS** IN YOUR TEETH!

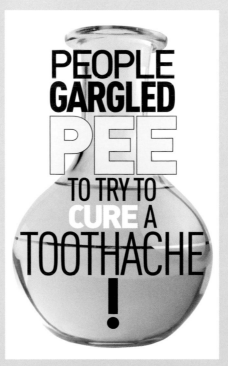

PEOPLE GARGLED PEE TO TRY TO **CURE** A **TOOTHACHE**!

SPIDER-WEBS WERE USED TO **CURE** WARTS.

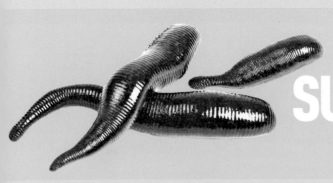

DOCTORS USED **LEECHES** TO **SUCK** **OUT THE "BAD BLOOD"** THAT THEY BELIEVED CAUSED THEIR PATIENTS TO BE **SICK.**

→ In some parts of South America, people **roast & eat** tarantulas.

→ The world's most **venomous** spider is the Brazilian wandering spider— it's **15 times** more venomous than a rattlesnake.

→ Spiders taste and smell through **organs** on their legs.

→ Fishing spiders can **float** on water.

THE GOLIATH BIRD-EATING SPIDER

is wider than a **basketball;** the world's **SMALLEST** spider is smaller than a **pinhead.**

→ Young spiders can **regrow** lost legs.

Empire State Building

Some visitors to New York City's famous landmark report a ghostly figure wearing bright red lipstick and 1940s clothing showing up in their photos. Others have seen her crying and heard her say her boyfriend was killed in World War II. They say she then passes through the side of the building, jumps, and disappears.

Spooky Vacations

EVEN IF YOU DON'T BELIEVE IN GHOSTS, THESE **SPINE-CHILLING** DESTINATIONS ARE ENOUGH TO GIVE ANY TRAVELER A GOOD **CREEP-OUT.**

Leeds Castle

This spooky castle in Kent, England, is supposedly home to a ghostly canine. But if you see this haunted hound, expect some bad luck. Legend says bad things happen after people see this phantom black dog.

Paris Catacombs

In the late 1700s, cemeteries in Paris, France, were overflowing with bodies. As a result, the dead were stored in tunnels under the city. This practice continued until 1860. Today, these creepy catacombs are a kind of art gallery featuring the bones of about six million people.

The *Queen Mary*

While carrying U.S. soldiers to Europe during World War II, the R.M.S. *Queen Mary* was in an accident that killed hundreds of people. Today the ship is used as a hotel in Long Beach, California, U.S.A.—but some guests still report hearing the haunting sound of the crash and its victims.

St. Augustine Lighthouse

A lighthouse that produces mysterious giggles? Ghostly faces appearing in windows? A strange lighthouse keeper in a blue uniform? That's what visitors to this lighthouse and museum in St. Augustine, Florida, U.S.A., have reported. Some think the strange sightings are related to a tragedy in the 1800s in which a cart tumbled into the ocean and killed three people who were in it.

The Pirates' House

Would you like a haunting with your dinner? At this restaurant in Savannah, Georgia, U.S.A., many diners report seeing and hearing ghost pirates from the 18th and 19th centuries, when the building operated as an inn and tavern. What can one expect from a restaurant in a place people call the most haunted city in the country?

THIS COUPLE HAS BEEN HOLDING HANDS FOR 1,500 YEARS.

EXPERTS think the man may have been **BURIED** looking at the woman, but **FLOODS** caused his head to turn away.

Namaqua Dune Mole Rat
<<<

WHERE IT LIVES: Namibia, South Africa

WHY IT'S AWESOME: This burrowing beast digs special chambers in its **underground** home. One is called a "bolt-hole," designed for the animal to **hide** in when it feels threatened.

CREEPY-
LOOKiNG Yet Awesome Animals

Goliath Beetle
<<<

WHERE IT LIVES: Africa

WHY IT'S AWESOME: This beetle is one of the **largest** in the world. It loves sugary **snacks** such as tree sap and fruits, which it gets by using its scary, sharp **claws** to climb tree branches.

<<< Bald Uakari

WHERE IT LIVES: Brazil, Peru

WHY IT'S AWESOME: Pronounced "Wakari," this monkey's **red face** is actually a sign of **good health.** A sick Uakari has a pale, **white** face.

WHERE IT LIVES: Indo-Pacific coral reefs

WHY IT'S AWESOME: To catch its prey, this weirdly colorful creature uses what looks like a **fishing rod** attached to its face. It **reels** in and eats meals in as little as seven milliseconds.

Painted Frogfish

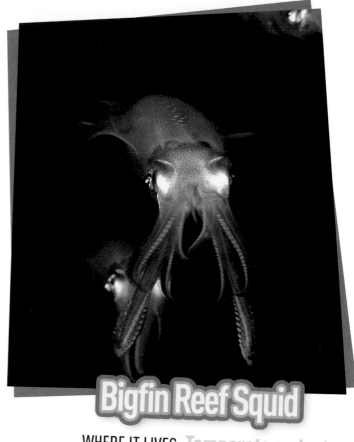

Bigfin Reef Squid

WHERE IT LIVES: **Temperate and tropical oceans**

WHY IT'S AWESOME: This squid rarely contracts **diseases,** so scientists use it to study **cancer prevention** and nutrition. Snorkelers can spot the **squid** off the shores of Hawaii.

Pygmy Seahorse

WHERE IT LIVES: **Indonesia**

WHY IT'S AWESOME: At nearly an **inch** (2.5 cm) long, this little sea creature can fit into the **palm** of a baby's hand.

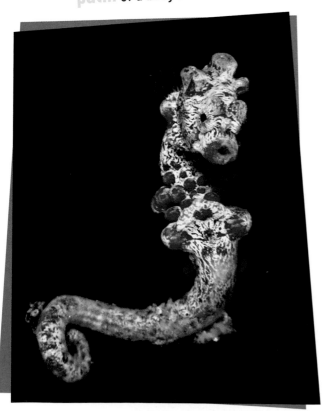

Dreadlocked Donkey

WHERE IT LIVES: **Europe, mostly France**

WHY IT'S AWESOME: In addition to having one of the **wackiest** hairdos in the animal kingdom, the Poitou is one of the world's **largest** donkey species and one of its most **endangered** livestock animals.

MESSAGES from your brain **TRAVEL** along your nerves at up to **200** miles an hour (322 km/h).

It takes major brainpower to make a call in São Paulo, Brazil, where an artist redesigned one of the city's phone booths. Head to page 136 to check out more weird art.

CHAPTER 7

WHAt's the DEAL?

IN INDIANA, U.S.A., IT IS ILLEGAL TO JOIN A MARCHING BAND PARADING DOWN THE STREET.

IT'S ILLEGAL TO ENTER THE BRITISH HOUSE OF PARLIAMENT WEARING A SUIT OF ARMOR.

YOU'RE BREAKING THE LAW IF YOU HAVE A PET SKUNK in NORTH DAKOTA, U.S.A.

IT'S AGAINST THE LAW TO HOOT LOUDLY AFTER 11 P.M. ON WEEKNIGHTS IN ATHENS, GEORGIA, U.S.A.

IN 1336 IT WAS ILLEGAL FOR MEN IN ENGLAND TO HAVE MORE THAN TWO COURSES AT A MEAL.

IT'S ILLEGAL TO FEED A WILD ALLIGATOR IN FLORIDA, U.S.A.

IT'S ILLEGAL TO DIE IN THE TOWN OF LONGYEARBYEN, NORWAY.

CHICKENS ARE NOT ALLOWED TO CROSS THE ROAD in QUITMAN, GEORGIA, U.S.A.

YOU ARE BREAKING THE LAW IF YOU BUILD A SAND CASTLE ON A BEACH in ERACLEA, ITALY.

IF YOU HAVE THE PLAGUE, YOU ARE NOT ALLOWED TO CALL A TAXI in LONDON, ENGLAND.

Robo Rickshaw >>>

Who needs a donkey when you've got a robot? A Chinese farmer built this rural robot from discarded metal, wire, screws, and nails. Powerful enough to pull a cart and a human, it is programmed to speak a sentence. And best of all, it can walk around for up to six hours before needing to be recharged.

Cool Inventions

THESE AWESOME
innovations could be in your future.

Grass Wheel

Don't live near a park? Don't worry! With the Grass Wheel, you can take a walk in the park anytime—and anywhere—you want to. This wooden orb, lined with soft green sod, acts as a giant hamster wheel for humans. That way, you can enjoy nature wherever you, uh, roll—no mowing required!

Mobile TV

Here's one way to share your favorite TV show with everyone you know: Just download the file, pop on one of these TV hats, and broadcast your program for all to see. Created by a company in Japan, these monitors are battery powered and come complete with an LCD dispay.

Leg Springs

You may not be able to leap tall buildings in a single bound like Superman, but with the help of Powerisers, you can come pretty close. These spring-loaded contraptions strap on to your feet and let you bounce, flip, and soar up to 16 feet (5 m) in the air.

Underwater Scooter

With the HydroBOB, you can be an underwater explorer without a mask, flippers, or mouthpiece. Use the handlebars to steer, press a button to keep the vehicle moving, and use its air bag to control depth. An onboard air tank allows you to breathe underwater for an hour, and the clear dome gives you a 180-degree view of your surroundings.

HIDE & SEEK

These wild animals really know how to take cover. See if you can spot these camouflaged critters in their natural environments.

NOW YOU DON'T

NOW YOU SEE IT

HORSING AROUND

WHAT IT IS: Pygmy seahorse

WHERE IT LIVES: Indonesia

COOL CAMO: Smaller than a penny, this mini-swimmer stays incognito underwater thanks to bumpy skin that matches the texture and the color of the coral in which it lives. It blends in so well that the species was only recently discovered by humans!

UP A TREE

WHAT IT IS: Scops owl

WHERE IT LIVES: Southern and central Africa

COOL CAMO: This tiny owl—about the size of a sparrow—hides from bigger birds by puffing up its gray and white feathers and perching against a tree trunk. It may also stretch out to the side to look like a branch.

NOW YOU SEE IT

NOW YOU DON'T

FLOWER POWER

WHAT IT IS: Orchid mantis

WHERE IT LIVES: Southeast Asia

COOL CAMO: With white or pinkish coloring and legs that look like flower petals, this insect practically becomes one with the orchids in which it tends to hide.

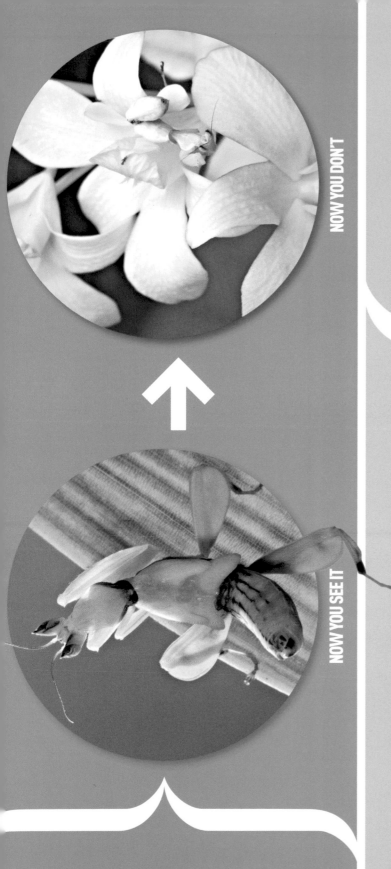

NOW YOU SEE IT

NOW YOU DON'T

SNEAK ATTACK

WHAT IT IS: Horned frog

WHERE IT LIVES: Indonesia, Malaysia, Singapore, and Thailand

COOL CAMO: This funky frog's brown coloring and horns help it stay hidden among leaves on the forest floor. That way, when it's time for a snack, it can sneak up on insects, snails, and smaller frogs that get close to its tongue.

NOW YOU SEE IT

NOW YOU DON'T

133

HAWKEYE also likes to **SWIM** in the **POOL** with her buddy **MUTLEY.**

The **CUSTOM SUIT**— which features a **BUBBLE-SHAPED** glass helmet and a mini-oxygen tank— cost more than **$15,000** to build.

Hawkeye's **OWNER** first **BUILT** a scuba suit for his **DOG,** Mutley.

HAWKEYE stays **UNDERWATER** in her backyard pool for up to **28 MINUTES.**

HAWKEYE THE CAT SWiMS IN THE WORLD'S FIRST FELINE SCUBA SUiT.

Even before diving, **HAWKEYE** was known to make a **SPLASH...** into the family **BATHTUB!**

THESE **COLORFUL CARS** "HANG OUT" ON A GIANT **CLOTHESLINE** >>> AT A FESTIVAL IN **ENGLAND.**

Weird ART

YOU **DON'T** HAVE TO BE EiNSTEiN TO MAKE A CALL FROM THIS **BRAINY** PHONE BOOTH IN <<< **BRAZIL.**

GOTCHA!

THIS GORILLA LOOKS LIKE HE'S **ESCAPING** FROM A PAINTING, BUT IT'S JUST AN **OPTICAL ILLUSION.** >>>

<<< A **JAPANESE ARTIST** USES A **TOOTHPICK & SPOON** TO **SCULPT** FACES FROM **BANANAS!**

THIS **DOUBLE-DECKER BUS** CALLED THE "LONDON BOOSTER" DOES **PUSH-UPS** WITH ITS **MUSCULAR** ARMS AND EVEN **GRUNTS** AS IT "EXERCISES." >>>

CLONE
HENGE

MORE THAN
800,000 PEOPLE
VISIT THE **REAL STONEHENGE**
EACH YEAR—HUNDREDS MORE
VISIT **WACKY REPLICAS** BUILT
AROUND THE WORLD.

FastFACTS

WHAT: Stonehenge, a 4,600-year-old man-made rock formation

WHERE: Salisbury Plain, England

MYSTERIOUS MONUMENT: No one really knows what the rocks are supposed to signify, but many people think they were originally a burial site.

LONG HAUL: Stonehenge was built in three stages over the course of 1,500 years.

HEAVY LOAD: The largest stone weighs as much as 50 tons (45 metric tons)!

Carhenge
WHERE: Alliance, Nebraska, U.S.A.
MADE FROM: 38 old cars lined up, shaped, and stacked to look like the real deal
FUN FACT: The cars are about the same size as the standing stones of Stonehenge.

Foamhenge
WHERE: Natural Bridge, Virginia, U.S.A.
MADE FROM: Blocks of Styrofoam painted gray
FUN FACT: The sculptor shaped and positioned each block just like the real Stonehenge.

Fridgehenge
WHERE: Santa Fe, New Mexico, U.S.A.
MADE FROM: Refrigerators
FUN FACT: No heavy machinery was used to create Fridgehenge—just simple tools such as ropes and pulleys.

Inflatable Henge
WHERE: U.K. (traveling)
MADE FROM: A 20-foot (6-m)-high inflatable bouncy castle
FUN FACT: It took two months to construct the springy replica of the ancient monument.

Cubehenge
WHERE: Traveling installation
MADE FROM: 116 colorfully lit cubes
FUN FACT: The light installation frames an outdoor dance floor.

<<< Shark Thief

WHERE IT LIVES: Off the coast of the **BAHAMAS**

BAD BEHAVIOR: After a scuba diver tried to **SNAP** shots of this 14-foot (4.3-m)-long tiger shark, the feisty fish **SNATCHED** the camera right from his hands and **SWAM** away!

>>>

Umbrella Snatcher

WHERE IT LIVES: **DUDLEY, ENGLAND**

BAD BEHAVIOR: During a **DOWN-POUR**, this lively lemur—who lives in a zoo—**GRABBED** an umbrella from a visitor and made a run for it. The visitor got **SOAKED!**

Animal
RASCALS

Meal Crasher

WHERE IT LIVES: **ASHBOURNE, ENGLAND**

BAD BEHAVIOR: This pet camel needs better table **MANNERS!** Every morning, he pokes his head through the **WINDOW** of his owner's house and joins the family meal. His favorite treat? **BANANAS ON TOAST!**

>>>

Big Gulper

WHERE IT LIVES: **ETALI SAFARI LODGE, SOUTH AFRICA**

BAD BEHAVIOR: Drink up! This **THIRSTY** elephant helped itself to a drink from this resort's **JACUZZI** while a surprised guest **SAT** just a few feet away.

Snack Sneaker

WHERE IT LIVES: **HERTFORDSHIRE, ENGLAND**

BAD BEHAVIOR: This big **BIG CAT** didn't seem to mind when a tiny **RAT** raided the jaguar's enclosure to **NIBBLE** on the cat's meaty meal.

Jewel Thief

WHERE IT LIVES: **ALBANY, GEORGIA, U.S.A.**

BAD BEHAVIOR: Mistaking **DIAMONDS** for doggie treats, Honey Bun the Pomeranian munched on **$10,000** worth of the gems at his owner's jewelry store. **NATURE** took its course and the diamonds were "returned" a day later.

CRUiSE
CONTROL

BALOO

THE CAR'S FRONT WHEELS ACT AS RUDDERS, HELPING IT STEER IN THE WATER.

THE AMPHICAR HAS A FOUR-CYLINDER SPORTS CAR MOTOR.

The Amphicar can "drive" on land and in the water!

YOU'LL NEED BOTH A DRIVER'S LICENSE AND A BOATING LICENSE TO DRIVE THIS CAR.

TWO PROPELLERS UNDER ITS BODY KEEP THE AMPHICAR MOTORING UNDERWATER.

FORMER U.S. PRESIDENT LYNDON B. JOHNSON PLAYED TRICKS ON FRIENDS BY DRIVING HIS AMPHICAR DOWN A HILL AND "CRASHING" INTO A LAKE WHILE SHOUTING THAT THE BRAKES WERE BROKEN!

AMPHICAR ADVENTURES

- Amphicar drivers have navigated the Yukon River and the English Channel, and motored to Santa Catalina Island, 22 miles (35 km) off the coast of California, U.S.A.

- The cars have been featured in at least four films.

- Amphicar owners gather together at annual "swim-ins" in Ohio, U.S.A.

- At least two U.S. presidents—Lyndon B. Johnson and Jimmy Carter—owned these aquatic autos.

7 Facts ABOUT THE STRANGEST

SOME **GOLF** COURSES HIRE SCUBA **DIVERS** TO FISH **BALLS** OUT OF THEIR **PONDS.**

PROFESSIONAL **SNAKE WRANGLERS** IN AUSTRALIA CATCH **SNAKES**

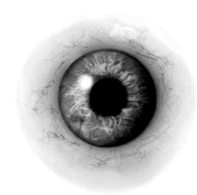

A **GERMAN MAN** MAKES **ARTIFICIAL EYES.**

THAT HAVE **SLiTHERED** INTO **PEOPLE'S HOMES.**

"**FORTUNE**

Jobs ON EARTH

SOME **WORKERS** AT A **MOUTHWASH** COMPANY HAVE TO **SMELL** PEOPLE'S **BAD BREATH**!

HUMAN "**FOOD TECHNOLOGISTS**" ACTUALLY TASTE CAT AND DOG **CHOW** FOR **PET FOOD** COMPANIES.

A **MAN** IN **ARIZONA**, U.S.A., MAKES A LIVING **HUNTING FOR METEORITES** IN THE **DESERT**.

"**WRITERS**" GET PAID TO CRAFT **MESSAGES** FOR **FORTUNE COOKIES**.

Apes
laugh
when
tickled.

A baby orangutan gets carried by its mom until it learns how to climb and swing by itself at about 18 months old. Swing over to page 155 for more facts about apes.

Eye
WONdER

To **CREATE** this modern "light painting," the photographer traced the surface in his kitchen with an **LED LIGHT** on a dark background.

DON'T WORRY! The person on the floor is not hurt. This is the photographer's **WIFE** posing for the picture.

THE **ART** OF light PAINTING

STARTED MORE THAN

100

YEARS AGO.

Set on an extra-slow shutter speed, the camera shutter stayed open for **24 MINUTES** to capture the path of the moving light.

Funny Hotel Room

>>>

WHERE:
Berlin, Germany

WHY IT'S WACKY:
Every corner and angle in this colorful room in the Arte Luise Kunsthotel is **outlined** with a thin, hand-drawn black line, making you feel like you're part of an actual **comic strip.** That will keep you laughing!

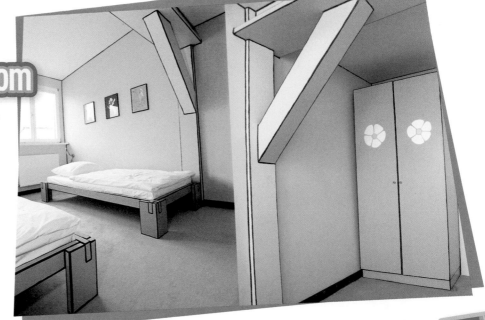

World's WACKIEST Buildings

Elephant Building

WHERE:
Bangkok, Thailand

WHY IT'S WACKY:
This **32-story** skyscraper is built in the shape of Thailand's national animal, the elephant! **>>>**

Underwater Hotel

WHERE:
Fiji

WHY IT'S WACKY:
This planned hotel will feature an **all-glass suite** 40 feet (12 m) under the sea and access to your **own submarine!**

<<<

WHERE:
Suweon, South Korea

WHY IT'S WACKY:
This **$1.6 billion home**—featuring four deluxe commodes with automatically lifting lids—is part of a theme park.

Toilet House

Basket Case

WHERE:
Newark, Ohio, U.S.A.

WHY IT'S WACKY:
The **headquarters** of this basket manufacturer looks just like one of the products it produces—only it's **160 times larger!**

>>>

Tall Teahouse

WHERE:
Nagano, Japan

WHY IT'S WACKY:
It's no wonder that the name of this teahouse means **"too high"** in Japanese. It's perched atop two 20-foot (6-m)-tall tree trunks and is accessible only by ladders.

151

THE U.S. AIR FORCE ONCE HAD AN OFFICIAL **UFO AGENCY** CALLED PROJECT BLUE BOOK.

LEGENDARY **CHUPACABRAS** REPORTED IN MEXICO AND THE SOUTHWESTERN U.S.

—BLOOD-SUCKING MONSTERS MAY ACTUALLY HAVE BEEN COYOTES WITH AN UGLY-LOOKING SKIN DISEASE.

HUNDREDS OF **LARGE FOOTPRINTS** —ALLEGEDLY LEFT BY BIGFOOT— HAVE BEEN PHOTOGRAPHED.

A **SCULPTURE** OUTSIDE THE HEADQUARTERS OF THE **CIA,** A U.S. SPY AGENCY, CONTAINS **FOUR** DIFFERENT **SECRET CODES.**

PEOPLE IN THE UNITED STATES, SPAIN, AND RUSSIA REPORT MORE **UFO SIGHTINGS** THAN PEOPLE IN MEXICO AND GERMANY.

CRYPTOZOOLOGY

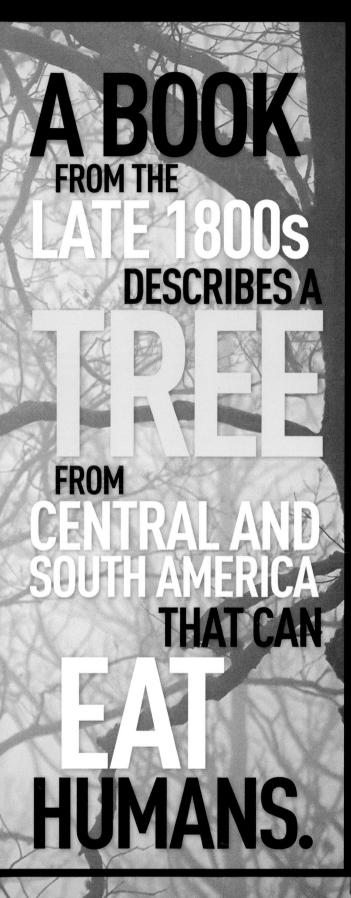

A BOOK FROM THE LATE 1800s DESCRIBES A TREE FROM CENTRAL AND SOUTH AMERICA THAT CAN EAT HUMANS.

SOME PEOPLE BELIEVE THAT A **GIANT ANACONDA**—THE YACUMAMA—LIVES IN THE AMAZON RAIN FOREST AND GROWS TO 150 FEET LONG. (46 m)

LEGEND HAS IT THAT A **5-FOOT-LONG** (1.5-m) ACID-SPEWING MONGOLIAN DEATH WORM LIVES IN THE GOBI DESERT.

IS THE STUDY OF "HIDDEN ANIMALS," SUCH AS THE LOCH NESS MONSTER AND THE ABOMINABLE SNOWMAN.

DOGS

only see **YELLOW,** blue, and **GRAY.**

MOST MONKEYS AND APES SEE IN FULL COLOR, LIKE HUMANS DO.

ultimate secret revealed!

Sure, your pet pooch loves chasing after his favorite red ball in your backyard.

But to him, the ball probably looks gray or black—and may be difficult for him to see against the green grass. That's because dogs have fewer types of retinal cones—special light-catching cells in the eye that respond to color—than most humans and other primates, such as apes and monkeys. Dogs see only a few hues and depend more on their superpowered sense of smell to detect objects. So when it comes to tracking down a red ball against the green grass, it's much easier for your dog to just sniff it out.

Upside-Down Eagle >>>

This eagle may look like it's falling out of the sky, but it's actually flying upside down! Eagles—which can dive at speeds of up to 100 miles an hour (160 km/h)—sometimes invert themselves for a mating ritual or to defend themselves from predators. Whatever the reason, people really flipped out when they saw this bird's acrobatics!

Amazing Animals!

WHETHER THEY'RE **SUPERSMART,** TOTALLY TALENTED, OR JUST **WILDLY FUNNY,** SOME CREATURES ARE SIMPLY INCREDIBLE. CHECK OUT THESE TRUE TALES OF **ANIMAL ANTICS!**

Walking Gorilla

Apes are rarely mistaken for humans, but when Ambam the western lowland gorilla stands upright and starts strolling around on his feet, he looks a bit like a big, hairy man. While most gorillas prefer traveling on all fours, Ambam, who lives in a zoo in Kent, England, often walks upright, his arms swinging by his sides. One big benefit to standing tall? He can see over the wall of his enclosure—and scope out when his keepers are bringing food!

<<<

Golden Zebra

Think zebras never change their stripes? Then take a look at Zoe, whose gold stripes (and bright blue eyes!) are a result of a genetic condition that causes a lack of pigment in the coat. Zoe, who lives in captivity, is one of just a few known "golden" zebras to survive beyond birth.

Surfing Alpaca

Pisco is believed to be the first ever surfing alpaca! These mountain animals—which are bred for their silky coats—are not known for their swimming skills. But that hasn't stopped Pisco from hopping on a surfboard in the Pacific Ocean. Pisco wears a life jacket while riding waves with his owner, who has also taught his dog, hamster, and cat how to hang…20!

Dressed-Up Ducks

Fashionable friends flock together! At least that's the case at the annual Pied Piper Duck Fashion Show in Sydney, Australia. Ducks waddle down a runway dressed in outrageous outfits, from cowboy costumes to whatever other styles fit the, uh, bill.

Brainy Bird

To reach nuts outside of his cage, Figaro the cockatoo snags sticks and makes tools to reel them in. He's the first known cockatoo to not only use but create tools to problem solve. That's one brilliant bird!

Real or Fake?

THESE WAX FIGURES OF BARACK AND MICHELLE OBAMA SURE LOOK REAL! FIND OUT THE TRICKY WAYS THAT MADAME TUSSAUD'S NEW YORK CREATED THIS SPITTING IMAGE OF THE FAMOUS COUPLE!

Red silk threads serve as **VEINS** on each **EYEBALL**.

Knotted **ROPE** creates the look of **VEINS** on the bodies.

Each strand of **HAIR** is inserted **INDIVIDUALLY**, a process that takes about five weeks to complete.

The figures get their washed and **MAKEUP** touched up regularly.

It takes **ARTISTS** approximately to create each sculpture.

The U.S. first couple's formal wear is **INSPIRED** by the outfits they wore to the 2009 Presidential Inaugural Ball.

The **FIGURES** are standing in a re-creation of the President's famous **OVAL OFFICE** in the White House.

The life-size figures were made **2 PERCENT** larger than the actual Obamas because

159

PEACOCKS CAN fan OUT THEIR TAIL FEATHERS AS WIDE AS A SOFA!

This **PEACOCK** was born with no pigment in its feathers, giving it an awesome **ALL-WHITE** appearance.

The peacock is the **NATIONAL** bird of **INDIA.**

White peacocks are born **YELLOW,** but turn white by the time they're **TWO.**

BABY peacocks are called **PEACHICKS.**

A **GROUP** of peacocks is called **A PARTY.**

WHITE peacocks are usually bred by humans who keep them as **PETS.**

9 COOL FACTS

AMAZON RIVER DOLPHINS ARE SOMETIMES BRIGHT PINK.

THE **HIMBA PEOPLE** IN NAMIBIA, AFRICA, HAVE **NO WORD** FOR THE COLOR **BLUE.**

THE **sky** ON **Venus** IS orange-red.

"NATIONAL SCHOOL BUS GLOSSY YELLOW" IS THE ACTUAL NAME OF THE PAINT COLOR USED ON **SCHOOL BUSES IN THE U.S. AND CANADA.**

ABOUT COLOR

SOME **WATERMELONS** ARE **YELLOW** INSIDE.

Some **chicken eggs** have **red yolks.**

NO COUNTRY HAS A **FLAG** WITH **PINK** ON IT.

SOME PEOPLE ONLY SEE IN **BLACK, WHITE, AND GRAY.**

MOOD RINGS CHANGE **COLOR** because of **TEMPERATURE,** not **MOODS.**

Hairy Car

NAME:
Instant No. 1

WHY IT'S WILD:
You might be tempted to **pet** this car, which an artist covered with thousands of **boar hairs.** He drives this four-wheeled fuzz ball—a mobile art piece.

NAME:
The Wind-Up

WHY IT'S WILD:
Built using the frame of a toy truck, this **pint-size ride** comes equipped with mirrors, windshield wipers, and working lights. Despite the Wind-Up's toylike name, it actually has an engine as powerful as a **motorcycle's.**

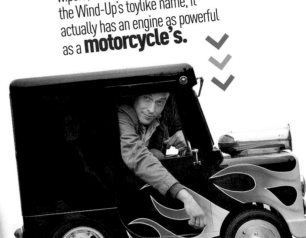

WiLD Rides!

Big Yellow

NAME:
BBC (Big Banana Car)

WHY IT'S WILD:
It's a 23-foot (7-m) **fiberglass banana** on wheels! Anyone have some ice cream and chocolate sauce?

Chair Lift

NAME:
Casual Lofa

WHY IT'S WILD:
◄◄◄ This **motorized sofa car** features a pizza pan steering wheel, a chocolate bar to change gears, and a working television. The couch can cruise at **87 miles an hour** (140 km/h) and was once considered the world's fastest piece of furniture!

Wacky Wagon

NAME:
Jeepney

WHY IT'S WILD:
These brightly painted buses were once **military jeeps,** but are now the main source of public transportation in the Philippines. The funny name is likely a mixture of "jeep" and "knee," because seating is **knee-to-knee** inside. ►►►

Buckle Up!

NAME:
Superbus

WHY IT'S WILD:
With 16 winglike doors, this futuristic ride looks more like the **Batmobile** than a bus. The luxury ride has room for **23 passengers** and can hit speeds as fast as a sports car! ►►►

A 10-foot (3-m)-wide **cowboy hat** sits atop this Eiffel Tower **replica** in Paris, Texas!

The design started out as a logo for a local radio station. Then a real tower was built outside a Paris, Texas, U.S.A., civic center. Find out about other wacky roadside attractions on page 172.

PARIS
Texas

CHAPTER 9

WILD WORLD

DUNG
BEETLES use the
STARS in the
MILKY WAY
as a **compass** at night.

➜ Why do dung beetles need GPS? It's important that they **roll** their **dung ball** in a **straight line,** or else another hungry beetle will steal their **smelly stash.**

→ Dung beetles can bury **250 times** their own weight in dung **in one day.**

→ Dung beetles can **see patterns of light** around the **sun, moon, and stars** invisible to the human eye.

→ When scientists placed **little hats** on the beetles to block their view of the **stars,** the beetles **rolled around aimlessly.**

→ These beetles **eat animal droppings!** Some hitch a ride on their favorite animal and wait…until **dinner is served!**

Avian Aromas >>>

MYTH: Mother birds will reject their babies if they have been touched by humans.

BUSTED! If a baby bird is returned to its nest by a human, the mother will probably not notice the smell of the human on the baby. Birds have a poor sense of smell. However, they have a great sense of sight!

Animal Myths Busted!

<<<< Clean Canines?

MYTH: A dog's mouth is cleaner than a human's mouth.

BUSTED! It all depends on what you mean by "clean." It's a close race between the number of bacteria in a human's mouth and in a dog's mouth. The important part, though, is that the types of bacteria in each species are different, so they really are a whole different animal.

That's Just Batty!

MYTH: Bats are blind.

BUSTED! Bats' eyes are small and sometimes poorly developed, but they work just fine. The saying "blind as a bat" refers to the fact that bats rely on a form of sonar, called echolocation, to avoid obstacles in the dark.

<<<

Scaredy-Birds

MYTH: Ostriches stick their heads in the sand when they are afraid.

BUSTED! Ostriches are slow runners, so instead of speeding away from danger, they flop to the ground and play "dead." From a distance, their light-colored head and neck look buried against the sandy ground.

Seeing Red?

MYTH: Bulls charge at the color red.

BUSTED! In traditional bullfighting, bulls have been known to charge at the red cape that is flashed in front of them. But it is the motion of the cape, not its color, that makes the bull charge with such fury.

<<<

Falling Felines

MYTH: Cats always land on their feet, unharmed.

BUSTED! Cats do have a tremendous ability to reposition their bodies in midair while falling. They are not always successful, however, and they are not always unharmed. And—you guessed it—they don't have nine lives!

<<<

WiLD ROADSiDE Attractions

Viking Ship

WHERE IT IS:
Amsterdam, **Netherlands**

WHY IT'S WILD:
This 50-foot (15-m) Viking ship is made of millions of **ice-cream sticks** and more than a **ton of glue.**

<<<

Eiffel Tower and Cowboy Hat **>>>**

WHERE IT IS:
Paris, Texas, U.S.A.

WHY IT'S WILD:
There are **nine American cities named Paris,** but this one knows how the famous European monument can be mixed with a little **homespun flavor.**

Dragon Statue

WHERE IT IS:
Yangzhou, China

WHY IT'S WILD:
This **towering** statue is nearly 98 feet (30 m) long, and is made from more than 2,800 **porcelain dishes** and cups.

<<<

WHERE IT IS:
Escondido, California, U.S.A.

WHY IT'S WILD:
This isn't your average park's sculpture garden. The **mosaic art** features a snake wall, **whimsical creatures**, and a 24-foot (7.3-m) Queen Califia, inspired by the state's mythical and cultural roots.

Queen Califia's Magical Circle

WHERE IT IS:
Atacama Desert, Chile

WHY IT'S WILD:
This 36-foot (11-m) concrete hand sticks out of the **driest desert** in the world.

Hand Sculpture

WHERE IT IS:
Mitchell, South Dakota, U.S.A.

WHY IT'S WILD:
Since 1892, **corn ear murals** have covered the outside of this building. They are replaced each year with a **new theme**, such as "Salute to Rodeo" and "Everyday Heroes."

Corn Palace

Turtle Sculpture >>>

WHERE IT IS:
Dunseith, North Dakota, U.S.A.

WHY IT'S WILD:
This turtle is made of more than **2,000** steel wheel rims. The head weighs more than a ton (907 kg).

THIS AUSTRIAN PARK TURNS INTO A LAKE FOR HALF THE YEAR.

The **CRYSTAL-CLEAR WATER** appears green due to the **GRASS** and **FOLIAGE** beneath the water.

Melting snow from the surrounding **MOUNTAINS** fills the lake up to **33 FEET** (10 m) in the late spring and early summer.

SCUBA DIVERS in the lake can see fish **SWIMMING** through tree branches and around park benches.

10 CRAZY FACTS

Ukrainians consider **spiders** and their webs **good luck,** so artificial ones are often used as Christmas decorations.

THE WORLD'S SMALLEST COUNTRY—VATICAN CITY, IN THE CENTER OF ROME, ITALY—IS ABOUT THE SAME SIZE AS AN 18-HOLE GOLF COURSE.

TO MAKE ROOM ON TOKYO'S CROWDED SUBWAYS "PUSHERS" ARE PAID TO SQUEEZE IN MORE PASSENGERS AND TO MAKE SURE THEY DON'T GET STUCK IN THE DOORS.

THERE IS A TOWN IN **WALES** CALLED LLANFAIRPWLLGWYNGYLLGOGERYCHWYRNDROBWLLLLANTYSILIOGOGOGOCH.

IN INDIA, THE ROOTS OF LIVE RUBBER TREES HAVE BEEN USED TO "GROW" A BRIDGE ACROSS STREAMS.

BECAUSE EARTH BULGES AT THE MIDDLE, MOUNT CHIMBORAZO in Ecuador is 1.5 miles (2.4 km) CLOSER TO THE MOON THAN EVEREST.

ABOUT COUNTRIES

THE **ALBANIAN** LANGUAGE HAS **27 WORDS** FOR DIFFERENT KINDS OF **MUSTACHES.**

LLAMA DROPPINGS ARE BURNED AS **FUEL** IN PERU.

LAKE RETBA IN SENEGAL IS BRIGHT **PINK.**

Dust from the **Sahara—** the largest hot desert in the world— **can travel** all the way to **North America** in about a week.

ENERGY FROM VOLCANOES IS HARNESSED TO **HEAT HOMES** IN ICELAND.

THE **INFINITY**

THE **HOTTEST** KNOWN **STAR**— AT 540,000°FAHRENHEIT— (299,982°F) IS **50 TIMES** HOTTER THAN OUR SUN.

JAPANESE **MACAQUES,** OR **"SNOW, MONKEYS,"** TAKE BATHS IN **HOT** SPRINGS.

HYDROTHERMAL VENTS CAN HEAT WATER TO **750**°F (400°C) AND SOME HAVE WEIRD NAMES LIKE **GODZILLA,** SNAKE PIT, AND HOMER SIMPSON.

POMPEII **WORMS**

LIVE AT THE BOTTOM OF THE OCEAN AND CAN **WITHSTAND** HIGHER TEMPERATURES THAN ANY OTHER ANIMAL, **up to 176°F.** (80°C)

CHILI, ONE OF THE WORLD'S HOTTEST PEPPERS, IS MORE THAN 250 TIMES HOTTER THAN TABASCO SAUCE.

IN THE HOT AUSTRALIAN DESERT, **KANGAROOS LICK** THEIR ARMS TO STAY **COOL.**

THE **SMELLY SKUNK CABBAGE PLANT** CAN CREATE ITS OWN HEAT—ENOUGH TO BLOOM IN THE WINTER AND MELT SNOW.

IN CALIFORNIA'S DEATH VALLEY IT WAS AT LEAST **100°F** (38°C) FOR **154** DAYS IN A ROW.

URANUS MAY CONTAIN **DIAMOND ICEBERGS** FLOATING ON LIQUID DIAMOND SEAS.

FaSHiON FUN

THE **SCOTLAND** TOURISM BOARD HOPES TO ATTRACT VISITORS BY MODELING **SHETLAND PONIES** IN HAND-KNITTED **WOOL SWEATERS.**

EVER FEEL THE COMPETITION **BITING** AT YOUR HEELS? YOU WILL IF YOU **WEAR** THESE **SHARK SHOES!**

WHEN DOES AN ORDINARY PAIR OF **JEANS** BECOME **EXTRAORDINARY?** WHEN THE LIGHTS ARE OUT AND THEY **GLOW IN THE DARK!**

THIS CHARITY WORKER FROM **LONDON, ENGLAND,** KNOWN AS **PEARLY KING,** GETS DECKED OUT IN A **SUIT OF BUTTONS** FOR A DAY ON THE JOB. >>>

EXPRESS YOUR <<< **INNER WOLF** BY WEARING THE LATEST HAT **FASHION** FROM DESIGNER **RYNSHU.**

^^ IS IT **ART** OR IS IT FASHION? **PUCKER UP** FOR A **KISS** FROM **CRAB LIPS** MADE FROM FACEPAINT!

>>> DESIGNED **FOR A DAY** AT THE ENGLISH **HORSE RACES,** THIS HAT WILL LEAVE YOU **HUNGRY** FOR A **PROPER BREAKFAST.**

SECRETS of the STATUE of LibeRtY

HER INDEX FINGER IS EIGHT FEET (2.4 m) LONG.

NOT VISIBLE FROM THE GROUND ARE CHAINS AND A BROKEN SHACKLE AT THE STATUE'S FEET.

WINDS OF 50 MILES AN HOUR (80 km/h) CAUSE THE TORCH TO SWAY UP TO SIX INCHES (15 cm).

IT'S POSSIBLE TO STAND ON THE TORCH, BUT IT'S BEEN CLOSED TO VISITORS SINCE 1916, WHEN A HUGE EXPLOSION OCCURRED NEARBY.

EACH EYE IS 2 FEET, 6 INCHES (.8 m) WIDE.

A COPPER SHEETING OVER THE STATUE IS THE THICKNESS OF TWO PENNIES.

FastFACTS

NAME: Statue of Liberty (aka Lady Liberty)

BIRTH DATE: Dedicated on October 28, 1886

HEIGHT: 111 feet, 1 inch (33.9 m) from heel to top of head

GIFT OF FRIENDSHIP: From France to the United States

SYMBOL OF: Freedom and democracy

INSPIRATION: Modeled after the Roman goddess of Liberty; face is said to resemble the sculptor's mother

FastFACTS

IS LADY LIBERTY A RESIDENT OF NEW YORK OR NEW JERSEY?

She lives in New York—sort of. Lady Liberty's home is on Liberty Island, which is U.S. federal property. The island is in New York Harbor, within New York State territory, even though it is closer to New Jersey.

THE STATUE SAT IN CRATES UNASSEMBLED FOR NEARLY A YEAR UNTIL A PEDESTAL WAS BUILT FOR HER TO STAND ON.

LADY LiBERTY WASN'T ALWAYS GREEN.

The **STATUE OF LIBERTY** is covered in 62,000 pounds (28,123 kg) of copper! The material starts out **THE COLOR OF A PENNY** but turns green over time.

SOME SCIENTISTS THINK
that by the year
2100,
we should be able to
TRAVEL THROUGH SPACE
at about **134 MILLION**
(216 million km/h)
miles an hour.

Some private **SPACE TRAVEL** companies are testing **aircraft** that would allow citizens to go on a spaceflight.

TICKET PRICE?

$200,000!

ultimate secret revealed!

How do scientists think we can make it to the stars and start living like characters in science fiction movies?

They think nuclear fusion would make this possible by the year 2100. Nuclear fusion is the energy source of hydrogen bombs and of the stars themselves. A nuclear fusion engine would be able to propel a starship up to 20 percent of the speed of light! With that kind of power, we could finally go hurtling toward the stars, ready to explore what's really out there.

fact finder

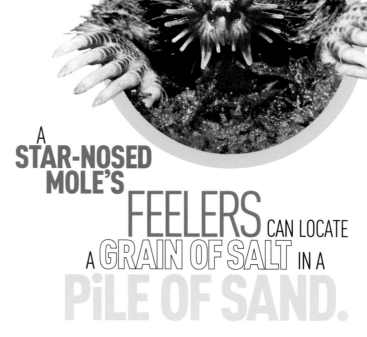

A STAR-NOSED MOLE'S FEELERS CAN LOCATE A GRAIN OF SALT IN A PILE OF SAND.

A THREE-STORY-TALL **EYEBALL SCULPTURE** WAS ONCE ON DISPLAY IN **CHICAGO, ILLINOIS, U.S.A.**

fact finder

AUSTRALIA'S **LARRY** THE **LOBSTER** STATUE WEIGHS ABOUT AS MUCH AS **2 GREAT WHITE SHARKS!**

fact finder

THIS **AMAZiNG** HOVERCRAFT **CAN FLY UP TO** 70 MiLES AN HOUR (113 km/h) **AND RIDE** **6-FOOT-TALL** (1.8-m) WAVES.

PEOPLE SPEND ABOUT $200 MiLLiON A YEAR ON **PET COSTUMES—** LIKE THIS ONE FOR **WILLIS** THE SUPERPUG!

credits

COVER AND FRONT MATTER

Cover (UPLE), Meredith Parmelee/Getty Images; Cover (UP CTR), Rex/Rex USA; Cover (UPRT), Kenneth C. Catania; Cover (LE CTR), Mike Greenslade/Australia/Alamy; Cover (LOLE), John Chapple/Rex USA; Cover (RT CTR), Hammacher Schlemmer/Rex/Rex USA; 2–3 (UP), Bobby Haas/National Geographic Stock; 4 (UPRT), Pornchai Kittiwongsakul/AFP/Getty Images; 4 (LO), AP Images/Joerg Koch; 5 (LE), © Ingo Arndt/Minden Pictures; 5 (RT), © Paige Thompson/Solent News/Rex/Rex USA

BACK COVER

(UP), Brooke Lewis/Dreamstime; (LO) Tyne News/WENN/Newscom

CHAPTER 1

6, Annette Redner; 8 (UP), AP Photo/Kerstin Joensson; 8 (LOLE), Annette Redner; 8 (LORT), Hiroya Minakuchi/Minden Pictures; 9 (UPRT), Rod Veal/The Orange County Register/ZUMAPRESS/Alamy; 9 (UPLE), Bryan Terry/©The Oklahoman; 9 (LORT), Pornchai Kittiwongsakul/AFP/Getty Images; 9 (LOLE), © SWNS; 10–11, AP Photo/Red Bull Stratos, file; 11 (INSET), Rex Features via AP Images; 12 (UPLE), STR New/Reuters; 12 (LOLE), Jill Fromer/Getty Images; 12 (LOrt), Eye Ubiquitous/SuperStock; 12 (UPRT), Byjeng/Shutterstock; 13 (UPLE), Logan Cramer III; 13 (LOLE), KidStock/Getty Images; 13 (UPRT), Blend Images/SuperStock; 13 (LORT), Reuters/Harley Palangchao; 14 (UP), EDPPICS/Bill Smith/Rex USA; 14 (CTR), Marco Secchi/Alamy; 14 (LO), David Moir/Reuters; 15 (UP), Tyne News/WENN/Newscom; 15 (CTR), Li Chunguang/Newscom; 15 (LO), Caters News Agency Ltd; 16–17, AP Photo/George Nikitin; 17 (UP), Iakov Filimonov/Dreamstime; 17 (LO), Robert Dutton/Dreamstime; 18 (UP), Brian A Jackson/Shutterstock; 18 (RT), incamerastock/Alamy; 18 (LOLE), Brad Calkins/Dreamstime; 19 (LE), Johnfoto/Dreamstime; 19 (UPRT), Mark Thiessen/NGS; 19 (UP CTR RT), Mark Thiessen/NGS; 19 (LO CTR RT), MASH/Getty Images; 19 (LORT), DeAgostini/SuperStock; 20 (LOLE), Pär Edlund/Dreamstime; 20 (LE CTR), Linda Bair/Dreamstime; 20 (UPLE), Steven J. Kazlowski/Alamy; 20 (LORT), Barcroft Media/landov; 20 (RT CTR), Sponner/Dreamstime; 20 (UPRT), Musat Christian/Dreamstime; 21 (UPLE), Jeff Pawloski/Barcroft Media/Landov; 21 (LE CTR), NaturePL/SuperStock; 21 (LOLE), Shawn Jackson/Dreamstime; 21 (UPRT), Helmi Flick; 21 (RT CTR), Hoberman Collection/SuperStock; 21 (LORT), Image Source/SuperStock; 22 (UP), Barry Bland/Alamy; 22 (LOLE), Solent News/Rex USA, 22 (LORT), Carlos Baez Castro/NOTIMEX/Newscom; 23 (UP), Alexander Remnev/Solent News/Rex/Rex USA; 23 (LE), AP Photo/Alexander Zemlianichenko Jr; 23 (RT CTR), Mark Read/Rex USA; 23 (LO), Pornchai Kittiwongsakul/AFP/Getty Images/Newscom; 24, Tim Kitchen/Getty Images

CHAPTER 2

26, Vivid Africa Photograhy/Alamy; 28–29, National News/ZUMApress/Newscom; 29 (RT), SeanPavonePhoto/Shutterstock; 30 (LE), Patrick Aventurier/Getty Images; 30 (RT), M & Y Agency Ltd/Rex USA; 31 (UP), AP Images/NASA, Nick Galante, PMRF; 31 (UPRT),Hammacher Schlemmer/Rex/Rex USA; 31 (LE), Beate Kern/Rex/Rex USA; 31 (LO), Aerofex/ZUMA Press/Newscom; 32–33, CB2/ZOB/WENN.com/Newscom; 34–35, Babak Tafreshi/Science Source; 36–37, © Lise Ann Strum; 38 (UPLE), Wolfgang Mayer/Waldseilgarten-Höllschlucht; 38 (RT), Reuters/Sebastien Pirlet; 39 (UP), Reuters/Vivek Prakash; 39 (CTR), Rex USA/Rex USA; 39 (LO), David Cannon/Getty Images; 39 (UPRT), AP Photo/MPL International Ltd/ho; 40–41, AP Images/Joerg Koch; 42 (UPLE), Bobby Bank/WireImage/Getty Images; 42 (CTR), Pima Air & Space Museum; 42 (LOLE), Carsten Reisinger/Dreamstime; 42 (LORT), © Joel A. Rogers; 43 (UPLE), Vivid Africa Photograhy/Alamy; 43 (UPRT), Tom Patton/Red Bull Content Pool; 43 (LO), Bhairav/Dreamstime; 44–45, NASA/JPL

CHAPTER 3

46–47, Philipp Nicolai/Dreamstime; 48 (UPLE), Philipp Nicolai/Dreamstime; 48 (LE CTR), Victor Zastol`skiy/Dreamstime; 48 (LO), Stuart Key/Dreamstime; 48 (RT CTR), Cammeraydave/Dreamstime; 49 (UPLE), Kelpfish/Dreamstime; 49 (LO), Jezper/Dreamstime; 49 (UPRT), Sergey Berezin/Dreamstime; 49 (CTR), Mike_kiev/Dreamstime; 50–51, Mike Johnson/SeaPics.com; 50 (LOLE), Chen Art/Shutterstock; 50 (LORT), Igor Sokolov/age footstock; 51 (UPRT), © Aditya «Dicky» Singh/Alamy; 51 (LOLE), IgorXIII/Shutterstock; 51 (LORT), Naasrautenbach/Dreamstime; 52 (LOLE), © Kippa Matthews/Rex/Rex USA; 52 (UP), © Solent News/Rex/Rex USA; 52 (LORT), © Maria J. Avila/MCT/Newscom; 53 (UPLE), © Richard Wintle/Rex/Rex USA; 53 (RT CTR), Andy Newman/AFP/Getty Images/Newscom; 53 (LO), © Ray Tang/Rex/Rex USA; 54–55, Sebastian/Dreamstime; 56 (UPLE), Alexander Cherednichenko/Shutterstock; 56 (LE CTR), George Grall/National Geographic Stock; 56 (LO), brulove/Shutterstock; 56 (UPRT), Eric Isselee/Shutterstock; 56 (RT CTR), Laborant/Shutterstock; 57 (UPLE), John Lindsay-Smith/Shutterstock; 57 (CTR), Tom Reichner/Shutterstock; 57 (LOLE), Tyler Olson/Shutterstock; 57 (UPRT), Eric Isselee/Shutterstock; 57 (LORT), cretolamna/Shutterstock; 58 (UP), cujo19/iStockphoto; 58 (LO), Elramon/Dreamstime; 58–59, Philipp Nicolai/Dreamstime; 59 (UP), Santos06/Dreamstime; 60 (LE CTR), Richard du Toit/Minden Pictures/National Geographic Stock; 60 (CTR), Paul Michael Hughes/Dreamstime; 61 (LE), Steve Allen/Dreamstime; 61 (LE CTR), Peter Zijlstra/Dreamstime; 61 (RT CTR), Charles Brutlag/Dreamstime; 61 (RT), Kris Holland/Dreamstime; 62 (LE CTR), © Caters News/ZUMAPRESS/Newscom; 62 (UP), © CB2/ZOB/WENN.com/Newscom; 62 (LO), © National News/ZUMAPRESS/Newscom; 63 (UPLE), © Paul O'Connor/Whitehotpix/ZUMAPRESS/Newscom; 63 (LE CTR), © Dan James/Caters News; 63 (UPRT), © Barbara Gindl/EPA/Newscom; 63 (LORT), © National News/ZUMAPRESS/Newscom; 64 (Back), Jacek Chabraszewski/Dreamstime; 64 (CTR), Peregrinext/Dreamstime; 64 (CTR), Anhong/Dreamstime; 64 (CTR), Fireflyphoto/Dreamstime; 64 (CTR), Isselee/Dreamstime; 64 (CTR), Alekss/Dreamstime; 64 (CTR), Aerogondo/Dreamstime

CHAPTER 4

66–67, Joe Parker/Breitling/Handout/ Reuters; 68–69, Solent News/Splash News/Newscom; 70 (UPLE), ChinaFotoPress/Getty Images; 70 (UPRT), AF archive/Alamy; 70 (LORT), REN NETHERLAND/Barcroft Media/landov; 70 (LOLE), REN NETHERLAND/Barcroft Media/landov; 71 (UPLE), REN NETHERLAND/Barcroft Media/landov; 71 (UPRT), REN NETHERLAND/Barcroft Media/landov; 71 (LORT), REN NETHERLAND/Barcroft Media/landov; 71 (LOLE), REN NETHERLAND/Barcroft Media/landov; 71 (LOctr), Allstar Picture Library/Alamy; 72–73, Joe Parker/Breitling/Handout/Reuters; 72 (INSET), Joe Parker/Breitling/Handout/ Reuters; 74 (UPLE), AP Images/ColorChinaPhoto; 74 (UPRT), Maks Narodenko/Shutterstock; 74 (RT CTR), Presselect/Alamy; 74 (LOle), Pan Xunbin/Shutterstock; 74 (LORT), Pan Xunbin/Shutterstock; 75 (UPLE), Christian Heeb/Getty Images; 75 (LE CTR), jurra8/Shutterstock; 75 (RT), Mahe Bertrand/Abaca/Newscom; 75 (LOLE), Brittny/Shutterstock; 75 (LOLE), Annmarie Young/Shutterstock; 75 (LOLE), Hong Vo/Shutterstock; 75 (LOLE), Sally Scott/Shutterstock; 76–77, Photo Researchers/Getty Images; 77 (UP), Science Photo Library/Alamy; 77 (LOLE), SSPL via Getty Images; 77 (LORT), David Longendyke/Everett Collection; 78 (UP), vario images GmbH & Co.KG/Alamy; 78 (LO), Karen Anderson Photography/Getty Images; 79 (UPLE), AFP/Getty Images; 79 (UPRT), Sven Hagolani/Getty Images; 79 (LOLE), Daniel L. Osborne/Detlev van Ravenswaay/Science Source; 79 (LORT), Ursula Sander/Getty Images; 80–81, Eye of Science/Science Source; 81 (UPLE), kamnuan/Shutterstock; 81 (UPRT), Dan Kosmayer/Shutterstock; 81 (LO), Sergey Peterman/Shutterstock; 82 (UP), Tim Stewart News/Rex USA; 82 (LORT), REN JF/EPA/Landov; 82 (LOLE), Stuart Hughes/Rex USA; 83 (UPLE), Rex/Rex USA; 83 (UPRT), Robert Anic/PIXSELL/Splash/Newscom; 83 (LOLE), MONIKA GRAFF/UPI/Newscom; 84–85, Ross Parry Agency; 85 (INSET), Marvel/Paramount/The Kobal Collection

CHAPTER 5

86–87, © Roland Weihrauch/epa/Corbis; 88 (UPLE), Richard Austin/Rex/Rex USA; 88 (LOLE), Reuters/Thomas Mukoya; 88 (UPRT), © Isobel Springett; 88 (LOLE), Associated Press; 89 (UP), Nathan Edwards/Newspix/Rex/Rex USA; 89 (LOLE), ©2013 SeaWorld Parks & Entertainment, Inc./Matt Marriott; 89 (LORT), © Rina Deych; 90–91, ©Richard Eriksson; 92 (LE), Monkey Business Images/Dreamstime; 93 (UP), Darko Plohl/Dreamstime; 93 (LE), Og-vision/Dreamstime; 93 (RT), Antonio Muñoz Palomares/Dreamstime; 94–95, Juliengrondin/Dreamstime; 96 (UPLE), Martin Garnham/Dreamstime; 96 (UPRT), Jurgen Freund/Nature Picture Library; 96 (CTR), Don Johnston/Getty Images; 96 (LO), GEORGETTE DOUWMA/Nature Picture Library; 97 (UPE), Viter8/Dreamstime; 97 (LOLE), © Steve Downer/ardea.com; 97 (UPRT), Associated Press/Ahn Young-joon; 97 (LORT), Kampee Patisena/Dreamstime; 98 (LO), National Geographic/Getty Images; 98 (UPLE), Jon Feingersh/Getty Images; 98 (UP), NASA/SDO; 98 (RT CTR), Daniel Loretto/Shutterstock; 99 (LO), Comstock/Getty Images; 99 (UPLE), Alex James Bramwell/Shutterstock; 99 (RT CTR), Carsten Peter/Getty Images; 99 (UP), Ed Freeman/Getty Images; 100 (UPLE), © Roland Weihrauch/epa/Corbis; 100 (LO), Courtesy VenusMommy; 100 (UPRT), Dante Fenolio/Getty Images; 101 (UP), Pemotret/Dreamstime; 101 (CTR), Natural History Museum/Rex Fea/Associated Press; 101 (LO), David Haring/DUPC/Getty Images; 102–103, Kim Taylor/Nature Picture Library; 103 (CTR), Susan Schmitz /Shutterstock; 103 (UPRT), Amlet/Dreamstime; 104–105, Trix1428/Dreamstime

CHAPTER 6

106–107, Oleg Kozlov/Dreamstime; 108 (UP), Joao Figueiredo/Flickr Open/Getty Images; 108 (CTR), © Helen Driggs KRT/Newscom; 108 (LO), John Block/Blend Images/Getty Images; 109 (UPLE), © Paul Grover/Rex Features/Associated Press; 109 (LOLE), © Richard Jones/Sinopix/Rex/Rex USA; 109 (UPRT), © Debbie Goard/Rex/Rex USA; 109 (LORT), © Chris Verraes/Rex/Rex USA; 110–111, Steve Gschmeissner/Science Photo Library/Getty Images; 112 (UP), Piotr WawrzyniukShutterstock; 112 (LO), Fotoeye75/Dreamstime; 113 (UP), © WILDLIFE GmbH/Alamy; 113 (LO), slon1971/Shutterstock; 114–115, sebra/Shutterstock; 115 (UPLE), Marinescu Lenuta/Dreamstime; 115 (UPLE CTR), Showface/Dreamstime; 115 (UPRT CTR), Feng Yu/Dreamstime; 115 (UPLE), Kalin Nedkov/Dreamstime; 115 (RT CTR), Maxfx/Dreamstime; 115 (LE CTR), Konstanttin/Dreamstime; 115 (LORT), Tracy Whiteside/Dreamstime; 115 (LORT CTR), Goran Turina/Dreamstime; 115 (LOLE CTR), Linncurrie/Dreamstime; 115 (LOLE),iko/Shutterstock; 116 (UPLE), Oleg Kozlov/Dreamstime; 116 (LO),3drenderings/Shutterstock; 116 (UP), © Forrest Smyth/Alamy; 117 (UPLE), Tatjana Baibakova/Dreamstime; 117 (LO),Galina Mikhalishina/Shutterstock; 117 (UPRT), Dusty Cline/Dreamstime; 117 (CTR), Zakaz/Dreamstime; 118–119, © Piotr Naskrecki/Minden Pictures; 119 Royalty Free; 120 (LO), Jyothi/Dreamstime; 120 (UP), Stuart Monk/Dreamstime; 121 (UPRT), Jonathan Weiss/Dreamstime; 121 (LE CTR), Thomas McConville/Photographer's Choice/Getty Images; 121 (LORT), © Vince Streano/Corbis; 121 (LO), Ptphotos/Dreamstime; 122–123, Ministry of Heritage and Culture and Superintendence for Archaeological Heritage of Emilia-Romagna/Rex/Rex USA; 124 (UP), © Bruce Davidson/Nature Picture Library; 124 (LO), © Ingo Arndt/Nature Picture Library; 124 (CTR), © Pete Oxford/Nature Picture Library; 125 (UPLE), © JurgenFreund/Nature Picture Library; 125 (LOLE), © Alex Mustard/Nature Picture Library; 125 (UPRT), © Constantinos Petrinos/Nature Picture Library; 125 (LORT), © Gavin Rodgers/Rex/Rex USA

CHAPTER 7

126, Yasuyoshi Chiba/AFP/Getty Images; 128–129, Bates Littlehales/National Geographic Stock; 130 (Up), Reinhard Krause/Reuters; 130 (LO), Andre Forget; 131 (UPRT), Oshiyuki Aizawa/Reuters; 131 (LOLE), Petr Josek/Reuters; 131 (LOCTR), Andrew Sneath/Solent News/Rex/Rex USA; 132 (UPLE), Tim Laman/naturepl.com; 132 (LE CTR), Travel Ink/Getty Images; 132 (RT CTR), Richard du Toit//Getty Images; 132 (LORT), age fotostock/SuperStock; 133 (UPLE), Bill Coster/ARDEA; 133 (LE CTR), Pascal Goetgheluck/ARDEA; 133 (RT CTR), Joseph T Collins/Getty Images; 133 (LORT), Chris Mattison/alamy; 134–135, Gene Alba; 136 (UP), Roger Bamber/Alamy; 136 (LO), Yasuyoshi Chiba/AFP/Getty Images; 137 (UPRT), Nicky Loh/Reuters; 137 (UPLE), Keisuke Yamada/Rex/Rex USA; 137 (LO), Al Khan/Demotix/Corbis; 138–139, Guy Edwardes/Getty Images; 139 (UPLE), Richard Ellis/Alamy; 139 (UPRT), Philip Gould/Corbis; 139 (LOLE), Rudolf Abraham/Alamy; 139 (RT CTR), Eye Ubiquitous/SuperStock; 139 (LORT), Luke MacGregor/Reuters; 140 (UPLE), Karin Brussaard; 140 (UPRT), DZG/Rex/Rex USA; 140 (LO), Mikael Buck/Rex/Rex USA; 141 (UP), Kerry Hardy/CATERS NEWS; 141 (CTR), © Casey Gutteridge/Solent; 141 (LO), Chuck Roberts; 141 (LO), Ksenia Romanova/Shutterstock; 142–143, Michele Crosera/Reuters; 144 (UPLE), Ingram Publishing/Alamy; 144 (LOLE), Lumina Imaging/Getty Images; 144 (UPRT), Gerry Pearce/Alamy; 144 (LORT), photastic/Shutterstock; 145 (LE), Accord/Shutterstock; 145 (UPRT), Nenov Brothers Images/Shutterstock; 145 (LORT), papa1266/Shutterstock

CHAPTER 8

146, Eric Isselee/Shutterstock; 149–149, Janne Parviainen/Rex/Rex USA; 150 (UP), Jagodka/Dreamstime; 150 (UPRT), Isselee/Dreamstime; 150 (CTR), Erik Lam/Dreamstime; 150 (LOLE), Isselee/Dreamstime, 150 (LORT), Roughcollie/Dreamstime; 151 (LO), Eric Isselee/Shutterstock; 151 (UP), Eric Isselee/Shutterstock; 152–153, Courtesy of Madame Tussauds, New York; 154–155, Paolo Cipriani/Getty Images, 156 (UPRT), Arte Luise Kunsthotel; 156 (LO), © Thailand/Alamy; 157 (UP), Splash News/Newscom; 157 (CTR), Ahn Young-joon/Associated Press; 157 (RT), © VIEW Pictures Ltd/Alamy; 157 (LO), KIICHIRO SATO/Associated Press; 158 (LO), Gareth Fuller/ABACAUSA.COM/Newscom; 158 (UP), Pam Mullins/Solent News/Rex/Rex USA; 159 (UP), Bill Adams MomentsNow.com/Getty Images; 159 (CTR), Paul Lovelace/Rex/Rex USA; 159 (RT), Reuters/Pilar Olivares; 159 (LO), © Alice Auersperg; 160 (UP), Top Photo Group/Rex USA; 160 (LO), © Liz O'Neill; 160 (CTR), AFP/Getty Images; 161 (UP), Patrick Barth/Rex USA; 161 (CTR), Per-Andre Hoffmann/Getty Images; 161 (LO), © Max Dereta; 162–163, Christian Handl Image Broker/Newscom; 164 (LE), Mark Carwardine/NPL/Minden Pictures; 164 (LO), Krischam/Dreamstime; 164 (CTR), AFP/Getty Images; 165 (UPLE), Anthony-Masterson/Getty Images; 165 (UPRT), Ingrid Prats/Dreamstime; 165 (LO), Shannon West/Shutterstock

CHAPTER 9

166, © Franck Fotos/Alamy; 168–169, © Mitsuhiko Imamori/Minden Pictures; 170 (LO), Willeecole/Dreamstime; 170 (UP), Wingkit/Dreamstime; 170–171 (CTR), Ivan Hlobej/Dreamstime; 171 (UP), Amskad/Dreamstime; 171 (UPRT), Ashley Whitworth/Dreamstime; 171 (LO), Samuha/Dreamstime; 172 (CTR), © Diederik Van Der Laan/EPA/Newscom; 172 (LO), © Franck Fotos/Alamy; 172 (UP), © Zhang Bingtao/Xinhua Press/CORBIS; 173 (CTR), © LHB Photo/Alamy; 173 (UPRT), © Rolf Haid/dpa/CORBIS; 173 (RT CTR), © Dennis MacDonald/Alamy; 173 (LORT), © Roadsideamerica.com; 174–175, © WaterFrame/Alamy; 176 (UP), Zigiz/Dreamstime; 176 (CTR), © Robert Harding Picture Library Ltd/Alamy; 176 (LORT), Mozzyb/Dreamstime; 177 (UPLE), Penywise/Dreamstime; 177 (UPRT), Bcbounders/Dreamstime; 177 (LO) © Hemis/Alamy; 178–179, © Valery Kraynov/Alamy; 180 (UP), © Kobi Levi/Solent News/Rex/Rex USA; 180 (LO), © Rob McDougall; 180 (RT CTR), © Naked & Famous Denim/Rex/Rex USA; 181 (UPLE), Victor Virgile/Gamma-Rapho via Getty Images; 181 (UPRT), © Bettina Strenske Image Broker/Newscom; 181 (LO), © Rex/Rex USA; 181 (RT CTR), © Paige Thompson/Solent News/Rex/Rex USA; 182–183, Leigh Warner/Dreamstime; 184–185, Space Art

BACK MATTER

186 (UPRT), Kenneth C. Catania; 187 (LORT), Rex/Rex USA; 188 (UPRT), Mike Greenslade/Australia/Alamy; 189 (LORT), Meredith Parmelee/Getty Images; 190 (UPRT), Hammacher Schlemmer/Rex/Rex USA; 190 (LOLE), John Chapple/Rex USA

PUBLISHED BY THE NATIONAL GEOGRAPHIC SOCIETY

John M. Fahey, *Chairman of the Board and Chief Executive Officer*
Declan Moore, *Executive Vice President; President, Publishing and Travel*
Melina Gerosa Bellows, *Executive Vice President; Chief Creative Officer, Books, Kids, and Family*

PREPARED BY THE BOOK DIVISION

Hector Sierra, *Senior Vice President and General Manager*
Nancy Laties Feresten, *Senior Vice President, Kids Publishing and Media*
Jay Sumner, *Director of Photography, Children's Publishing*
Jennifer Emmett, *Vice President, Editorial Director, Children's Books*
Eva Absher-Schantz, *Design Director, Kids Publishing and Media*
R. Gary Colbert, *Production Director*
Jennifer A. Thornton, *Director of Managing Editorial*

STAFF FOR THIS BOOK

Kate Olesin, Robin Terry, *Project Managers*
Mary Varilla Jones, *Release Editor*
James Hiscott, Jr., *Art Director*
Lisa Jewell, Kelley Miller, Jay Sumner, *Illustrations Editors*
Rachael Hamm-Plett, James Hiscott, Jr., Dawn McFadin, *Designers*
Ariane Szu-Tu, *Editorial Assistant*
Callie Broaddus, *Design Production Assistant*
Hillary Moloney, *Associate Photo Editor*
Sarah Wassner Flynn, Kathy Furgang, *Writers*
Julie Beer, Michelle Harris, *Researchers*
Michaela Berkon, Carly Larkin, Riley Kirkpatrick, *Editorial Interns*
Grace Hill, *Associate Managing Editor*
Joan Gossett, *Production Editor*
Lewis R. Bassford, *Production Manager*
Susan Borke, *Legal and Business Affairs*

PRODUCTION SERVICES

Phillip L. Schlosser, *Senior Vice President*
Chris Brown, *Vice President, NG Book Manufacturing*
George Bounelis, *Vice President, Production Services*
Nicole Elliott, *Manager*
Rachel Faulise, *Manager*
Robert L. Barr, *Manager*

The National Geographic Society is one of the world's largest non-profit scientific and educational organizations. Founded in 1888 to "increase and diffuse geographic knowledge," the Society's mission is to inspire people to care about the planet. It reaches more than 400 million people worldwide each month through its official journal, *National Geographic,* and other magazines; National Geographic Channel; television documentaries; music; radio; films; books; DVDs; maps; exhibitions; live events; school publishing programs; interactive media; and merchandise. National Geographic has funded more than 10,000 scientific research, conservation, and exploration projects and supports an education program promoting geographic literacy.

For more information, please visit www.nationalgeographic.com, call 1-800-NGS LINE (647-5463), or write to the following address:
National Geographic Society
1145 17th Street N.W.
Washington, D.C. 20036-4688 U.S.A.

Visit us online at nationalgeographic.com/books

For librarians and teachers: ngchildrensbooks.org

More for kids from National Geographic: kids.nationalgeographic.com

For information about special discounts for bulk purchases, please contact National Geographic Books Special Sales: ngspecsales@ngs.org

For rights or permissions inquiries, please contact National Geographic Books Subsidiary Rights: ngbookrights@ngs.org

Hardcover ISBN: 978-1-4263-1358-5
Reinforced Library Binding ISBN: 978-1-4263-1359-2
Scholastic edition: 978-1-4263-1628-9

Printed in the United States of America
13/RRDW-CML/1

ANATOMY OF A WEIRD BUT TRUE FACT

How does a fact make it into a Weird But True book?

First, it has to be **WEIRD.** Our team of editors and writers scour the news, the latest discoveries, Internet gems, crazy conversations, urban legends, wacky myths, and tantalizing tidbits to find a fact that's really weird.

It also has to be **TRUE.** So our team of researchers checks every single word to make sure the fact is 100 percent accurate.

It has to **LOOK COOL.** Our photo editors and designers find the perfect weird picture or the most dazzling weird design to make each fact jump out at you.

It has to **BE FUN.** Then we put it all together in a sensory overload presentation to knock your socks off.

Here's a weird-but-true fact about *Ultimate Weird But True 2:* It took an ultimate team of 5 editors, 2 writers, 3 designers, 3 photo editors, 2 researchers, plus lots of experts to make the weirdest, truest, most ultimate book around.